What Happened to My Little Girl?

Other Books by Nancy Rue

FOR TWEENS

On Authenticity

Everybody Tells Me to Be Myself, But I Don't Know Who I Am

Dear Nancy

The It's MY Life Book

The Creativity Book

The Uniquely Me Book

The Fun-Finder Book

The Sophie Series, fiction, Books 1–12

The Lily Series, fiction, Books 1–14

On Beauty

The Skin You're In

Dear Nancy

The Beauty Book

Here's Lily, fiction, Lily Series Book 1

The Lucy Novels, fiction, Books 1–4

On the Changing Body

Body Talk

Dear Nancy

The Body Book

Lily Robbins, M.D., fiction, Lily Series Book 2

Sophie's Secret, fiction, Sophie Series, Book 2

Lucy Out of Bounds, Lucy Novels, Book 2

On Relationships

Girl Politics: Friends, Cliques, and Really Mean Chicks

Dear Nancy

Moms' Ultimate Guide to the Tween Girl World

The Buddy Book

The Best Bash Book

The Blurry Rules Book

The Lily Series, fiction, Books 1–14

The Sophie Series, fiction, Books 1–12

The Lucy Novels, fiction, Books 1–4

On Spiritual Formation

The FaithGirlz Bible (edited by Nancy Rue)

That is SO Me: A One-Year FaithGirlz Devotional

The Year 'Round Holiday Book

The Values and Virtues Book

The Lily Series, fiction, Books 1–14

The Sophie Series, fiction, Books 1–12

The Lucy Series, fiction Books 1–4

For Teen Girls

Motorcycles, Sushi, and One Strange Book

Boyfriends, Burritos, and an Ocean of Trouble

What Happened to My Little Girl?

Dad's Ultimate Guide to His Tween Daughter

Nancy Rue with Jim Rue

ZONDERVAN®

ZONDERVAN.com/
AUTHORTRACKER
follow your favorite authors

We want to hear from you. Please send your comments about this book to us in care of zreview@zondervan.com. Thank you.

ZONDERVAN

What Happened to My Little Girl?
Copyright © 2011 by Nancy Rue

This title is also available as a Zondervan ebook.
Visit www.zondervan.com/ebooks.

This title is also available in a Zondervan audio edition.
Visit www.zondervan.fm.

Requests for information should be addressed to:

Zondervan, *Grand Rapids, Michigan 49530*

Library of Congress Cataloging-in-Publication Data

Rue, Nancy N.
    What happened to my little girl? : Dad's ultimate guide to his tween daughter / Nancy Rue with Jim Rue.
       p.   cm.
    ISBN 978-0-310-28472-7 (softcover)
    1. Fathers and daughters — Religious aspects — Christianity. 2. Preteens. 3. Girls — Psychology. 4. Girls — Conduct of life. 5. Girls — Religious life. 6. Parenting — Religious aspects — Christianity. 7. Child rearing — Religious aspects — Christianity. I. Rue, Jim. II. Title. III. Title: Dad's ultimate guide to his tween daughter.
    BV4529.17.R84 2010
    248.8'45 — dc22   2010051063

Scripture quotations marked *The Message* are taken from *The Message.* Copyright © 1993, 1994, 1995, 1996, 2000, 2001, 2002. Used by permission of NavPress Publishing Group.

Scripture quotations marked NIV are taken from the Holy Bible, *New International Version*®, NIV®. Copyright © 1973, 1978, 1984 by Biblica, Inc.™ Used by permission of Zondervan. All rights reserved worldwide.

Published in association with the literary agency of Alive Communications, Inc., 7680 Goddard Street, Suite 200, Colorado Springs, CO 80920. www.alivecommunications.com

Cover design: *Gayle Raymer Design*
Interior design: *Sherri L. Hoffman*

Printed in the United States of America

11 12 13 14 15 16 /DCI/ 24 23 22 21 20 19 18 17 16 15 14 13 12 11 10 9 8 7 6 5 4 3 2 1

For all the dads of mini-women,
and, of course, for Marijean . . .
and Baby Maeryn

Contents

1

Can Somebody Tell Me
What's Going On?

What Just Happened?

You come home from work the way you've done every night of her nine-year life, pretty much whipped but still ready for her to belt out of her room, eyes dancing, arms open, squealing her girl-child squeal. It is a sound only dogs can hear. Dogs and daddies.

You turn on your laptop, pour the usual cold whatever, and wait for the welcome. Whether you're likely to scoop her up and make an obnoxious noise into her neck, high-five her, or simply say, "Hey, Baby Girl, where's your mother?" you at least secretly savor the fact that *somebody* is ecstatic to see you no matter how you smell or who you've impressed or what you earned that day.

Yeah, so, where is she? No door has burst open. No flip-flop-clad feet have flapped down the hall. You do hear muffled squealing coming from the direction of her room, yet you have the immediate sense that it's directed not at you but at the other squealers who are obviously in there with her. Sounds like there's a platoon of them.

Mystified, if not slightly miffed that your arrival hasn't been heralded, you head for her doorway, already picturing her leaping up from her pile of stuffed animals and chirping, "Daddy! I didn't hear you come in!"

But the door is closed, and the cutesy pink-and-purple sign her mother bought at some froufrou boutique, proudly declaring this to be Her Room, has been replaced by one scrawled in Magic Marker on a piece of your laser printer paper. It says:

Out of the Mouths of Mini-Women

Sometimes my dad's all like, "You're growing up," and even starts crying a little. And other times? He treats me like a baby. Can't he just pick which one?

9

Girls only!
Boys stay out!

Snickering, you turn the knob and poke your head in.

The squealing chokes itself out. Four ponytails swish as faces turn toward you. Faces that look vaguely familiar, although you're sure you've never seen those particular lips gooey with color or those eyelids smeared with a shade of blue you haven't witnessed since your mom wore it in the '80s. You can pick out your daughter because hers is the mouth that opens and says,

"Da-*ad*! Didn't you read the *sign*?"

"Yeah," you manage to say, as your gaze takes in the tumble of MP3 players and polka-dotted journals and what even you recognize as your wife's old makeup bag. Where are the Barbie dolls? The tea set? The crayons in every color known to man?

"Hell-o-o!" your daughter says, hands on hips you weren't aware she had. "You're a *boy*!"

You think you might grin, might even say something clever and giggle-producing. But then she does a thing you could not have foreseen, even in the darkest colic-screaming, tantrum-throwing days of her baby- and toddlerhood.

She rolls her eyes at you.

Right up into her head. The thought comes to you that she must be having a seizure before you realize that this is merely the universal signal for "You just don't *get* it."

Whether you respond by backing out of the room or sending the friends home to their own fathers so you can ground her for the rest of her childhood or warn her that if she rolls her eyes at you again you're going to roll her head—your existence has been rocked. In that instant you know that you no longer automatically trigger, "Stop the world—there's Daddy!"

You might tomorrow. You might even later that evening when the other goopy-lipped girls have departed and she once again climbs into your lap. But you'll never again take that for granted, because, Dad . . . your daughter is now a tween.

What's a Tween?

Tween is a term coined by the advertising world to designate a kid between the ages of eight and twelve. One group of youth marketers actually calls them "the great tween buying machine."[1] Most of us look at them less as potential consumers than as children who are no longer sweet little baby people but who have not completely lost their minds yet and become teenagers. They are definitely "between" innocent childhood and confused adolescence, a station in life you'd think would be pretty easy, fairly carefree. You should have as few worries and hang-ups as they do.

Until the mid-twentieth century, even psychologists would have agreed with that. The in-between years were often referred to as the "latent" period, and parents tended to let out a four-year-long sigh of relief as they steeled themselves for the teen years everybody kept warning them about. It wasn't unusual to be enjoying a day at a theme park with your eight-year-old and have somebody turn to you in line and say, "You're having fun now, but wait till she gets to be a teenager."

But our view of the tween years has changed, and not just because marketers decided to give them a name and prey on their $43 billion annual spending power.[2] (An impressive sum for people who can't even drive themselves to the mall.) We're realizing that (a) a heck of a lot of important stuff is going on during those years, and (b) as parents we'd better jump on that because society already has. Those same marketers who named them "tweens" have also fashioned the acronym KGOY—Kids Getting Older Younger. Their sales campaigns for everything from shoes to breakfast cereal are based on the belief that ten is the new fifteen.

And then there's you, the dad, looking at your eight-, nine-, ten-, eleven-, or twelve-year-old daughter and saying, "Are you *serious*? She's still a little girl!"

Yeah. Try telling her that when the clothes on the store racks look like junior hooker wear and her friends are sniffing at her and saying, "You still play with *dolls*? What a baby." Inform her that she's a little girl when she drags home a backpack full of homework, when the gymnastics teacher tells her she needs to lose that baby fat if she's serious about the Olympics, when she starts her period at age ten—and even at that, she's a good six months "behind" her BFFs.

Child development hasn't changed. Eight- to twelve-year-olds are still on the same place on Maslow's hierarchy of needs where they've always been. It's society that's been altered—in some ways for the better, in some for the worse.

On the better side, we've come to realize that the tween years *aren't* latent, nor are they merely a rest period before teen hormones reach their peak. We know, in fact, that more physical, emotional, and mental development occurs during this period than in any other in their lives except birth to one year. Armed with that information, we can pay more attention to what's going on with our kids and direct how they grow from it, rather than assume this is just the calm before the storm, and that at age thirteen all hell is going to break loose.

Fathers of teen daughters have a huge influence on how that goes down. Huge. The good news is that you still have enough sway with that mini-woman to guide her into adolescence as a strong, confident, authentic, God-centered human being. The bad news? If you do nothing—and let's face it, that's easy to get away with—you direct her path too. She enters her teen years feeling unsure of who she is, insecure about her strengths, and doubtful in her faith. Dude, a big, big part of it is on you.

If you've even picked up this book and gotten to this point, it's obvious you want to have that positive influence as a dad. Either that or your wife has threatened you with eternal dinner-less-ness if you don't read it. You are probably already taking a real good stab at being a great girl-dad, maybe even better than you think. But chances are you're parenting that girl-child the only way you know how . . .

Christian author Terry Esau is the father of a tween daughter, and he lights up more when he talks about her than when he's telling you about his latest book. He says, "As a parent you tend to gravitate toward the way you were raised. It's like there's a hook in you, pulling you where you don't want to go."[3]

Not that there weren't wonderful dads in the '70s and '80s. Paternal instincts rank right up there with women's intuition and can shape awesome fathers. Always have. Typically, though, the grand-fathers of today's tweens (your dads) were the earliest of the Baby Boomers, born between 1945 and 1955, and were focused on making a living and dealing with tumultuous decades of war, racial tension, and changing moral values. They had to basically re-raise themselves in a society where nothing was as it had been when they were kids. Your dad's parenting style may have ranged from leaving it all up to Mom to running the whole show with an iron hand. In any case, it wasn't the norm for Dad to be involved in his children's lives the way Mom was.

However that affected you as a growing-up boy, it has more than likely influenced your parenting style too. You may hear yourself saying stuff to your kids you swore would never come out of your mouth because you hated it when your father said them to you:

"Because I said so."
"Stop that crying or I'll give you something to cry about."
"Don't make me stop this car."

Or, if you were raised in the South, "I'm fixin' to bust me some butt."

You were never going to yell at *your* offspring or make them live in fear of the dreaded "wait till your father comes home" or give them the occasional grunt from behind the newspaper and call it a conversation. Yet here you are, wincing every time you realize you've done all of the above or shrugging and saying, "No wonder my dad did that. Kids can drive you nuts."

In a new society, we owe it to our tween daughters to form our own style of parenting, one that matches the kind of growing up our girls are doing. A growing up that is far different from ours.

That's what this book is about. It's not an exposé on the mistakes our moms and dads made. In fact, we're all about encouraging you to keep the good stuff that shaped you into the great guy you are and toss out the things that aren't working any better for your kid than they did for you. It's not too late to do that. A tween girl isn't going to say, "Oh, so NOW you want to spend time with me? Forget it—I have my own life!" Wait till she's a teenager, though, and you might hear that and worse.

Nor is this book designed to make you feel guilty or change your personality (like it *could*) or tell you flat out how to be a father to your daughter. It's not a how-to book. It's more like a travel guide. We'll tell you what we know about the girl world you've found yourself in and give you suggestions for doing more than merely survive it. Just because you really *have* no authentic choice but to immerse yourself in it, understand it, and guide your daughter through it doesn't mean you can't have a great time while you're there. That's what we're about.

About Us

Now would be a good time to mention who "we" are and explain where we get off giving you all this advice.

One of us is Nancy Rue, tween girl "specialist." (I hate the word *expert*. Works for wine, ballistics, or rock climbing, but not for kids. Especially girls.) Nancy's been working with eight- to twelve-year-old girls for twenty years and has written 108 books (this is number 109), most of which are for and about that age group. She speaks extensively to tween girls and their moms about everything from puberty to leg shaving, mean girls to who-in-the-world-am-I? Her latest book is *The Mom's Ultimate Guide to the Tween Girl World* (Zondervan, 2010), which does for mothers what we hope this book will do for you. If your daughter's mom doesn't have that book, by the way, we strongly suggest that you pick it up so the two of you can be on the same page. Literally. At least 80 percent of Nancy's career time is spent blogging for, emailing with, talking to, writing for, and delighting in tween girls. She can tell you more than you really want to know.

While Nancy did much of the writing and research you'll find here, the narrating voice is mine—Jim Rue. My credentials are experiential. Not only have I fathered a daughter—now thirty-one and pretty amazing—but I've worked with the giggly, squealy female set as a camp counselor, music- and drama-camp director, youth-group leader, children's theatre director, youth-group adviser, and mission-trip team leader. I was everybody's "other dad" during our daughter's tween and teen years and am still known as Papa Rue by some who now have kids of their own. My success in those areas wouldn't be at all impressive (and maybe it still isn't!) if my life before all of that hadn't been in the military. I served as a SEAL for twenty-five years in active and reserve duty. With a background like that, being a dad to a tween girl was a challenge.

We're not the last word in raising daughters, which is why in the pages that follow we'll refer to other specialists and dads who've been where you are. You can't have too much information and support as far as we're concerned. More importantly, we'll talk about God's place at the center of all this, which is not an easy thing to grasp when your ten-year-old has told you that you just don't *understand*, and you're inclined to agree with her. More on all of that below. First, though, let's take a look at who a tween girl is and what makes her tick (you off!).

Here's the Deal

According to the U.S. Census Bureau, there were 20 million tweens in the United States in 2009 (a number that is projected to reach 23 million by 2020).[4] We can assume that approximately half of them are girls. What we can't assume is that they're all alike. It boggles the mind to think that there are 10 million different little personalities, but there you are. Kind of eradicates the tendency to lump them all together. But there are a few major characteristics you're going to find in any girl between the ages of eight and twelve, even though these same traits may express themselves differently in each tween. It's a good idea to get your mind around these. In fact, ignore them at your peril.

She knows everything. Everything. Her favorite sentence, in fact, is "I *know*." She's not being a little snot when she says that (okay, maybe she is, depending on whether she punctuates the sentence with an eye roll). She has merely discovered that she has a mind of her own and that she really does know a lot. At least, a lot more than you think she does.

I wish my dad knew how embarrassing it is when he does something that makes everybody look at him. Last Sunday, he yawned in church. Really loud. I had to put my bulletin in front of my face so nobody would see how red it was. Why does he have to do stuff like that?

She's active. Even if she's not into soccer or gymnastics, she probably can't sit still for long. She even stands on her head when she's reading a book. If she's a couch potato at this point, have her checked out by a doctor. Seriously.

She's confident and assertive. There's a range involved there. Your daughter may be quiet, shy, reserved, but that isn't necessarily a painful thing for her during the tween years. She's fine standing back and observing until she gets the lay of the land without worrying that everybody thinks she's a loser. If you have one on the other end of the scale — extroverted, opinionated, never met a stranger — you already know she'd be as comfortable meeting the First Lady as she is telling you how the household ought to be run.

Her emotions are at full tilt. Again, that runs the gamut from internalizer to full-blown drama queen, but the feelings are there, and they often run rampant because she doesn't quite understand them yet. As a rule, everything's either wonderful or horrible, with not much in between. She may not voice that, but if you're at all observant (that is, if you pull yourself away from the playoffs now and then), you'll see that emotional yo-yo in action.

She's not sure if she's a little girl or a pint-sized teenager. Which means her sophistication level on any given day (or hour) is unpredictable. After all, she doesn't just wake up the morning she turns thirteen and say, "Okay, time to start acting like an adolescent." One minute she's wailing that she wants to wear makeup and high heels, the next she's putting them on her Barbie doll. She's attached to her iPod — until you put on a Disney movie for her little sister and she's all over it. You're an embarrassment to her when you show up unexpectedly on her turf; don't appear for her soccer games and dance recitals, and you're toast.

She has a major balancing act going on. She's teetering on a line between:

Family	and	BFFs
Fitting in	and	Being an individual
Wanting security	and	Wanting to make decisions
Family values	and	Consumer culture

Eighty-five percent of the 1,223 tween respondents in a recent *Youth Trends* interview study said their family is the most important part of their lives, and that Mom and Dad are among their BFFs.[5] (You *do* know that means "Best Friends Forever," right?) Yet according to that same study, the average tween spends 12.1 hours a week watching TV and 7.3 hours online. Between that, school, other activities, and sleep time, your daughter spends less time hanging out with you than she does doing anything else. In fact, one father's research shows that the average American father spends less than ten minutes a day with his daughter.[6] No wonder the teetering is so precarious at this age.

Those are the typical tweenisms specialists concur on. Then there are the ones shared by the dads we've talked to. You know you're living with a tween girl when:

You need a guidebook to eye rolling.
The difference between a crying jag and a fit of giggles is undetectable.
You just got a lot stupider.

Maybe you had sisters growing up. Maybe you noticed some of that in them. Probably you didn't, since you had your own issues (playing third base, blowing up stuff with your chemistry set, mastering the fart sound with your armpit and a cupped hand—the important things in life). If you did happen to pick up on their fears, confusion, and anxiety (or you remember any of your own), multiply that by about five hundred to account for the very different world your daughter is living in. This is what that world looks like.

She's more connected technologically—and maybe less so personally. According to a Nielsen study, the average American tween (not teen) sends 1,146 text messages every month. That's four every hour they're not in school.[7] Girls this age are known to sit side by side in the back of a minivan and text each other. No joke. If your daughter has a Nintendo DSi, she can play games like Tinkerbell, Littlest Pet Shop, and Fashion Show, linking up with a friend and having a conversation without actually speaking, even though they're in the same room. It's rare to see a gang of tween girls playing hopscotch on the driveway or riding bikes to the park, ponytails flying. What self-respecting father would let his daughter play out in the open unsupervised like that? You can't just ignore reports of kidnappings and abductions, can you?

She's being exposed to a lot of information your generation didn't know about at eight and nine years old. She can flip through the channels during prime time and hear people talking about (if not actually doing) everything from masturbation to cocaine abuse. If she's listening to just about anything but Christian radio, she's going to hear language ranging from F-bombs on down. Not that she doesn't also hear it on the playground at school — even Christian school. You might be able to shelter her from all that, but she's still exposed to billboards every time you drive her down the highway. The ones showing adults in various forms of undress are bad enough, but she's also likely to see girls her own age being sexualized. One dad reports seeing an ad showing two tween girls in bikinis on a water buffalo; he was baffled as to how that tied in with the jewelry store chain it advertised.[8]

Marketers are now developing products for tweens specifically to make them feel older and more sophisticated, like their teenage sisters (who aren't necessarily ready for that either). One father of a tween daughter refers to them as products guaranteed to grow your girl up into a shallow bimbo. He was referring to a girls' pink piggy bank, with the words "Boob Job" on it, shown on a website featuring items for their rooms. We've heard of an online game called "Miss Bimbo." Flavored deodorant for nine-year-olds (one wonders why they need a deodorant at all, much less one that tastes good) with names like "Pink Crush" and "XOXO." Video games in which the choices are *ask Dad for money*, *gossip*, *date*, *meet girlfriends for lunch*, *shop*; the tween player knows she's won when she gets a boyfriend.

That trend is probably most apparent in the entertainment industry. According to Robert Beeson, founder of Essential Records, the tween market increased 38 percent in 2009, the only segment of the music industry that grew.[9] The Disney empire has taken tween marketing to a whole new level. Preteens are now the music industry's main target audience.

The effect of all that? The tween girl is influenced to scorn symbols of her immaturity—dolls, pretend games, age-appropriate dress, G-rated movies. She thinks she's supposed to be cool, flirtatious, trendy, and overly concerned with the way she looks. That expectation is hard enough for a girl at fourteen and fifteen. A tween is much "wobblier" than an adolescent. She relies far more on other people to tell her who to be and how to understand the world and find her place in it. She may have far too much power she isn't ready for.

Forget "sugar and spice and everything nice." Tween girls are being encouraged by not only the media and the advertising world but by their coaches, their teenage sisters, and often even their moms to develop "girl power." This is not healthy empowerment that allows her to become strong and confident, but the ride-roughshod-over-everybody (especially males) brand. She's told to fight for anything she wants, when she still doesn't know exactly *what* she wants. She translates that as "I get to be as bad as I want to be. There are no limits on me." Chances are, your daughter has either adopted that, or she feels like there's something wrong with her because she can't do it. In either case, that's a lot for a ten-year-old to handle.

The news is not all bad, Dad. Your tween daughter's world is an improvement over the premillennial one in many ways, and so is her generation. Today's tween girls are more comfortable as a whole with diversity. They're more family oriented than Generation X (born 1961–81). The current economy promises to make them less materialistic and consumer driven. Already, "being smart" and "protecting the environment" are among the things they think are "cool."[10]

The best news comes from the Girl Scout Research Institute, which in December 2009 released the results of its recent study of the ethical beliefs and values of tweens today and how they've changed since the 1989 study.[11] A few highlights to pull you out of that cave you want to crawl into (the 1989 findings are in parentheses):

> 62 percent said they would not cheat on a test (48 percent).
> 58 percent said they would refuse an alcoholic drink if offered one at a party (46 percent).

I wish my dad spent more time with me and gave me more attention. Last night he told my brother a story. He spent like twenty minutes by him and two minutes by me. Unfair is a word I'm familiar with.

It's kinda hard for us to have THAT good of a relationship when my dad has to help my brother, who's only a little bit younger than me, so he's now getting to be a "man" and needs my dad. I don't think my dad has time to care much about me personally.

33 percent said they would wait until marriage to have sex (24 percent).

84 percent said they will vote in every election (77 percent).

79 percent said they will volunteer in their community (a question not even asked in 1989).

79 percent said they would express an opinion they knew to be unpopular (72 percent).

26 percent said they feel pushed to fit in (34 percent).

94 percent say they have an adult in their lives who cares about them, and 92 percent of those said that adult is their parent.

62 percent said their parents were the first people they turned to for advice.

According to those findings, there is more going in her favor, and yours, than there is against. But that won't last for her indefinitely. She'll face worse as a teenager. Time is *not* on your side, and there's a lot to be done.

Where Do I Come In?

The first thing to establish in answering that question—where do I come in?—is that you *do* figure into your tween daughter's life in a far bigger way than you may realize. If you have sons, you know you have a powerful influence on them. You're their role model. So much of what kind of men they'll become depends on you. What you might be unaware of is that you have just as much influence on the kind of woman your daughter will grow into. You are not the "backup parent" who only steps up when Mom is about to flush said child down the toilet. Nor are you what one dad calls just a "walking wallet,"[12] whose sole job is to provide for the family and dish out funds when that tween plays her Daddy's Girl card. Here's the role *you* play—and no matter how you perform it, it makes a difference to her.

As your tween daughter is figuring herself out, your "masculine way of being in the world"[13] is appealing to her. She's not as limited at this age by what society says girls can and can't do as she'll be made to feel she is in the future. She can be whoever she wants to be right now, and you are the one who shows her how awesome it is to be strong, fast, smart, and decisive. What you do is pretty interesting, while Mom's typical activities—taking everybody everywhere, throwing kids into the bathtub, scrambling to get meals on the table—often aren't as exciting. Even if you do your share of those things, you do it in a man way that is fascinating to your daughter. This could be the easiest time in her life for you to relate to her, while you're still cool.

She's vulnerable to stress in a world that's fast and noisy and full of pressures, especially in school and other performance activities. She needs somebody to back her up when that world asks too much, when it's unfair, even when it's cruel. That somebody is Dad. We're not being sexist. Mom can do that too, but she's going to come in with the feminine values of caring, connection, relationship, and nurturing. You've got to join Mom to promote self-confidence, problem-solving, decision-making, goal-setting—all the stuff Mom learned from *her* father or from a woman whose feminine and masculine traits were well-balanced. Let's face it, guys, we're still dealing with a society that tries to cut women off from their power to be themselves. Your daughter needs both of you to model the courage to speak with her own voice.

Go figure—messages about appropriate dress and modesty (that is, not leaving anything to the imagination with her attire) are usually absorbed better coming from Dad than from Mom. That depends, of course, on your approach, which we'll get to later. At the very least, she needs a united front with both parents agreeing on reasonable limits that don't involve the girl dressing like a prairie wife. Without you in the picture, you could be looking at a mother-daughter power struggle. Only you can be believed when it comes to how boys react to half-clad classmates.

YOU are the one who shows her how she should expect to be treated by men. Her mother can talk about that until she develops laryngitis, but the proof that she's telling the truth (which is less and less a given as your daughter nears adolescence)—that comes from how you treat your wife *and* your daughter. We'll talk about that at length in chapter 7. For now, just know that your attitude toward women is

Out of the Mouths of Mini-Women

I never have the feeling my dad really knows me or understands me. He believes that Mom is there to raise me and my sisters and help us through problems.

not escaping your daughter for a moment. Your every move is getting into that little female head in spite of any attitude she's trying out on you. You are setting the standard. And we're not even going to say, "No pressure." It's on.

Being included in your world makes her feel valued. As our own daughter has told us in her adult years, "I knew early on that Mom's love was just there, no matter what I did. Dad's love was unconditional too, but I always felt like I wanted to impress him more. When I did, it wasn't like, 'Of course.' It was like, 'Yes. I'm special.'" Your daughter may not be able to verbalize that now, but if you *aren't* sharing your life with her—really sharing, not looking up occasionally from Craig's List and saying, "That's great, honey"—it's taking its toll on her already.

What You'll Find Here

As we've said, raising a daughter is huge. Which is why we aren't going to just dump it here for you to sort out. We've got a plan.

We've divided the above into six major areas of influence you have in your daughter's life—the things she cares most about right now.

Chapter 2, "What Happened to My Little Girl?" deals with *the physical changes* your daughter is experiencing. These are things that make you go "What?" when your wife says she's taking your baby out to buy her first bra. Think of it as everything you wished you'd known about the girl-thing when you were twelve. We'll walk you through the biology and give you a tutorial on how you can help your daughter develop a positive body image. As in, she won't grow up to constantly ask her husband, "Does this make me look fat?"

Chapter 3, "She'll Be Crying in a Minute," discusses *the mood situation* that accompanies the onset of hormones—when they are at their most confusing for everybody concerned. We'll help you keep the roller coaster from going off the tracks.

Chapter 4, "We Need Another Bathroom," tells you what you can expect on *the beauty front* (if you aren't experiencing that already). We'll give you some guidance in determining how involved you need to be in not only setting limits but in making sure your daughter knows she is uniquely beautiful.

Chapter 5, "Who Is She Today?" will educate you on your daughter's challenges in *finding her authentic self* in a cookie-cutter society. Our intention is to help you get her started on that journey. And to help you keep your sanity along the way.

Chapter 6, "Dealing with Girl Drama," will enlighten you on the world of *girl politics, RMGs (Really Mean Girls), and cyberbullying.* We'll sort through the differences between boys and girls in this arena and help you decide if, when, and how to intervene should things get ugly.

Chapter 7, "I Liked It Better When Boys Had Cooties," talks about the impending entrance of *boys* on the scene (if they have not already elbowed their way in, the little . . .). We'll offer advice on helping your daughter understand how she should be treated by a man and when she can expect that to happen. You'll get some encouragement in helping her navigate the world of absurd little creeps (tween boys) she is now annoyed and tormented by.

You'll see the same features in each chapter, so you'll know what's coming at you at any given moment.

What Just Happened? will start every chapter with a dad-daughter scenario. Sometimes these will be composites of actual situations; sometimes they'll be drawn directly from Jim's experience. In either case, you'll get the real deal. We hope you'll be able to relate.

Here's the Deal will walk you through the topic, giving the basic concepts, some statistics, and what the specialists have figured out for you. We won't bore you with a lot of psychobabble—just real stuff that will turn some lights on for you and help you see the effect you can have in this particular area.

In Reality is a quick way for you to assess where your daughter is on the topic and how you're handling it so far. Women typically love quizzes in magazines; you're not going to find them in *Sports Illustrated.* These aren't multiple-choice tests to determine your D.Q. And they're totally nonjudgmental. They're mostly just checklists that give you a chance to find out where you stand.

My dad is a really great guy and I know he loves me. But I've never really trusted him with my feelings because he yells at me a lot.

Learning from the Master turns to God as Father. You may be as surprised as we were to learn that the Bible doesn't say a whole lot about how to be a good father, so we basically have to take our cues from a day-to-day relationship with the Ultimate Parent. If you aren't a church-going dad, don't skip this part. We promise: no spiritual mugging.

Where Do I Come In? comes closest to a travel agenda. We'll give you options for putting all that information into practice using your own parenting style, including how to keep your sense of humor and enjoy your daughter, even as you maintain appropriate authority.

You'll also see some sidebars, quick shots that we hope will go deep. Consider them your Cliff's Notes. In **Out of the Mouths of Mini-Women**, you'll find quotes about dad stuff from tween girls Nancy has worked with. Get ready for in-your-face honesty. **Don't Say It, Dude** will keep you from alienating your daughter—*and* her mother—and prevent you from feeling like a jerk later on. **Bridging the Gap** is a prompt to pray that God will bridge the gap between what your tween daughter needs and what you have to give, because, Buddy, no matter how much you learn from this book, you can't do it alone.

Ground Rules

Since guys don't like to be told the same thing over and over (which according to Nancy they could avoid by actually responding the *first* time ... but that's for another book)—we're going to lay out some basics that apply to whatever issue we're exploring. They're like your default, so that even if you forget some of the particulars, you can find your way back to these and figure out what you're doing.

Yelling doesn't work. Not for the long haul. It might clear the room or bring sullen silence in the vehicle, but as far as a relationship goes, it's your least effective means of communication. Trust me. I did my share of it. But I have to tell you, the times when I sat down with my daughter (in the midst of her testing me to see how much I'd let her get away with) and said, "What are we doing here? What's going on?"—we were much more successful in working things out. The veins in your neck don't have to bulge for your daughter to know who's in charge. It's a matter of asking yourself how *you* want to be talked to and talking to *her* that way. You'll get that same respect in return. Ditto for criticizing, sarcasm, and lectures of longer than three minutes.

Answer her questions. "Go ask your mother" isn't the answer we have in mind (unless the question is about where something is, which you, as a male, never seem to know). Neither is "You shouldn't even be thinking about that stuff right now." This is a curious and confusing age for your daughter, and she wants answers. If she doesn't get them from you, she's going to seek them from somebody else—somebody who's infinitely less reliable than you are. Her BFFs. The boy-creature who sits next to her. The teenage babysitter. The Internet. If you don't have time for a discussion, make a date for later. If you don't know, tell her you'll get back to her and then do. If you don't take the time to answer—or you make her feel like a ditz for not knowing—she'll stop asking. At least, she'll stop asking *you*. Maintain your role as her go-to guy.

If you say no, have a reason. "Because I said so" doesn't count. Okay, yeah, there are instances when you have to say, "Do it and I'll explain later." As long as you make that happen at the next possible opportunity. Definitely teach her how to ask "why" respectfully. Don't let her put you on the defensive. Be proactive: "I'm going to have to say no to that, and here's why." With some daughters, you have to put a limit on the amount of time you spend stating your case, lest you be there until she starts college. Still, if you make sure she knows your answer is final and you're just doing a courtesy by backing it up, you won't find yourself arguing or justifying or debating. I was known to say, "No, Marijean. I have a bad feeling about it," and I think it taught her to trust her own instincts when she was the one making a decision.

If you're still not convinced, consider the amount of rebellion you want to deal with later, when she's a teenager. Teens don't just rebel because they're teenagers and they've heard they're supposed to. And they don't really rebel against the rules themselves, because they know there have to be some. They rebel against the person who makes the rules without reason, love, and respect. Save yourself and your daughter a whole lot of heartache and let her in on your rationale.

Spend time with her. Real time. Not "You watch your movie while I check my email" time. When we asked tween girls to say what one thing they wished their dads knew—this is only a sampling of their responses—

> *My dad gets up really early and comes home kinda late and watches TV for the rest of the night and checks his email like ten trillion times. Sometimes I wish I could hang out with him like he was my friend, but he just doesn't have time ...*
>
> *I wish he didn't have to work so much. I know it's for us, but I just wish he was there more. Really there ...*
>
> *I wish he would understand that I WANT to spend time with him. Can't he work ME into his schedule?*
>
> *My dad hardly has any time to play anything or TALK to me. If I do talk to him, he either says, "Go away," because he's working on the computer, or he'll say, "Maybe later," and he never gets to it. It makes me mad and sad ...*
>
> *My dad spends about an hour checking emails and looking on Craig's List. I wish he would just stop sometimes and ask about me or if I want to have a talk.*

I've noticed a common thread between our dad posts, and that's time. It seems like the girls whose dads spend lots of time with them have good relationships, and vice versa.

Here's the thing about that undistracted, one-on-one focus they want. Men aren't really multitaskers. We just aren't. We're more what therapist Don Elium calls single-focus thinkers.[14] There's nothing wrong with that while you're taking down a tree with a chain saw or piloting an F-15. It's a problem, though, when you promise your daughter a date at McDonald's and then make a few phone calls while she eats her McNuggets. She gets the message that she's in the way, a pain in the neck, not terribly interesting. She wonders what she did wrong and what she has to change to get your attention. Low self-esteem isn't far behind.

HOW to spend time with her? You no longer have to sit at a tea party table with your knees up to your ears, sipping imaginary tea and chitchatting with the teddy bear across from you. Your daughter is turning into an interesting person, so find out what she likes these days and do it with her. We're not talking toenail painting or mind-numbing shopping (unless you're into that). Look for common ground. Do you both like soccer—playing or cheering for the team? Whipping up homemade pizza for the rest of the family? Growing veggies? Fishing? Bike riding? Cutthroat Scrabble? Volunteering at the soup kitchen? It doesn't matter if you just take her for ice cream after dance class. Girls want fathers to be part of their lives.

If she shows any interest at all in something *you* do, draw her in. When I was getting my technical theater degree, Marijean was all about the drawings I did in set design and would spend hours on the floor of my study doing her own while I was at the drafting table. When I was mastering rock climbing for the Navy Reserves, I took her with me when I practiced and taught her the basics. Her mom had zero interest in snow skiing   even though we lived thirty minutes from Lake Tahoe—but Marijean wanted to go with me and turned out to be a natural. Basically, your tween will try anything if you encourage her and do it with her. I see it this way: it's your responsibility to get this child the best education possible, and so much of what she learns doesn't happen at school. Marijean got her nose under the hood when I was tinkering with the car and wanted to know how an engine ran; she currently knows more than her husband does about their vehicles. She had to be in the kitchen when I was making pancakes (secret family recipe which I will give up for a fee) and is now one of the better cooks around. Hey, you're a fool if you don't take the time. I still beat myself up over the instances when I could have and didn't. Being included in your world makes her feel valued and competent and confident.

If it sounds like you're going to have to quit your job to make this happen, relax. We know all of that can't go on daily. What *can* is eating dinner together regularly—the whole family—as opposed to grabbing fast food on the fly between ball games and dance lessons and church activities. Spend fifteen minutes with her at bedtime. Ask her to ride with you to the hardware store, and let her choose the radio station. Invite her to come talk to you while you shave. Roll your eyes *with* her when you catch that stupid TV commercial for the hundredth time. Have your own "things." (Mine with Marijean was,

"Hey, Mar—be careful out there" when I dropped her off at school.) Even the smallest exchange can have a huge impact.

Acting out always means something. Some of it's hormones, which we'll talk about in chapter 2, but you can't blame it all on that any more than you can attribute every dirty look you get from her mother on PMS. The reasons for a sudden regression to pitching a hissy fit are myriad, but one thing you can count on: if you lose her trust, her belief that you're going to be there for her, and she doesn't think she can depend on you, she's going to keep trying things until she believes in you again. Are you going to try to talk to her even when she puts a big KEEP OUT sign on her door? Are you still going to love her if she brings home a D- in math? Will she still be your princess if she says, "Du-uh, Dad"? We're not saying let her get away with that. We're saying look into what's going on, because she's still not mature enough to say, "Dad, you're not spending enough time with me and I'd like to rectify that situation." When you think about it, who is?

Show her who God is by living your faith. Living it, not working it. It's easy to let church work or your ministry become more important than your family. One well-known Christian counselor told us that many ordained pastors and spiritual "celebrities" come for parenting help after they've bought into the mentality that they're doing God's work, so God will take care of their kids' needs. The deal is, your daughter's view of God comes in part from what kind of father *you* are. Ask any woman who struggles with God as Father why that concept is hard for her. Let your daughter see your faith in action. Even when you don't have all the answers (not "if," but "when"), demonstrate that you're looking for them in God.

Listen. "Uh-huh" while you're scanning your iPhone for messages isn't going to cut it. Looking into those bright shiny eyes and soaking her in while she goes on—and on—and on—that's listening. Marijean would come home with all this misinformation from her friends—"Dad, did you know that yadayadayada"—and I'd cut her off with, "No, I didn't, because that's ridiculous." Next time I got in her face with a lecture, her eyes would glaze over, and I'd feel like I was looking in a mirror. Listen up, and for Pete's sake, don't act bored. Ninety percent of what she goes on about will probably be

Out of the Mouths of

Mini-Women

I wish my dad would listen to what I have to say. He assumes . . .

forgettable. It's that 10 percent you don't want to miss. The part where she says, "Ashley's sister says everybody has sex before they get married now. Do you think that's true?" Her ideas about things change almost daily, so don't assume you already heard this yesterday and tune out. If you ignore her now, she won't come to you later with questions you want input on: "What would you think about me getting married ... going to Africa ... joining the Army?"

Choose your battles. Just because everything is monumental to her right now doesn't mean it has to be to you. Decide what matters and let the other stuff work itself out. Seriously, is the state of her bedroom going to determine whether she gets into Princeton? Does that fit of giggles she had in church really mean she has no reverence for the Lord? Do you actually expect her to *not* scream at her little brother when she discovers he has flushed her diary down the toilet? Treating you and her mother with respect, being civil to her siblings (most of the time), doing her reasonable share around the house—those are things worth honing in on.

Tell her you love her. You can show her all you want, but she needs your words too. She needs to *hear* it from you. That includes genuine praise—she'll see through token approval and reward you with the now infamous eye roll—and encouragement—a critique of her every move on the way home from the soccer game won't improve her game. And while we're on the subject of talking, make sure she knows, from your own mouth, what your clear, reasonable expectations are and how they're going to be upheld.

One more ground rule, and this one may be the hardest to follow—

Try your hardest not to be overprotective. That's a subjective term, but we define overprotective this way:

Keeping your daughter completely sheltered from the world.
Rescuing her from every tough situation.
Making all her decisions for her so she won't fail or be hurt.
Fixing her problems for her or always telling her how to do it.
Constantly hovering and checking her progress.
Continually judging and criticizing so she'll get it right.

Out of the Mouths of Mini-Women

I want to be able to relate to my dad with some things, have privacy, and be able to talk to him about stuff I want to talk to him about. Like have my own life, but he still has authority.

Out of the Mouths of

Mini-Women

I hate it when my dad treats me like a baby. He won't even let me go to school, because he thinks they'll teach me about not believing God and make me think that people came from monkeys and other stuff. I think he needs to trust me that I'll be faithful in God.

The problem with the urge to be overprotective is that it comes from your deep love for your daughter—and yet it can do equally deep damage. Yeah, you need to shield her from the real danger and stand up for her when she's attacked and pull her out of potentially harmful situations. You just have to be careful not to consider dangerous and harmful everything that is not overtly Christian or that has anything to do with boys or that may result in her making a mistake and having to take the consequences. If you do, you're depriving her of the chance to learn how to make decisions, weighing those consequences for herself before she acts.

Right now, there are a lot of situations she faces where, if she does make the wrong choice, the results may be painful to her, but they aren't life threatening or even life altering. When she's a teenager, that changes. She'll be confronted with choices that could indeed endanger her life or her future. Should she get in the car with a kid who's been drinking? Should she just taste a little alcohol and see what it feels like? Should she go just a little further with that boy who says he loves her? Should she go into a sketchy part of town to try to help a friend who's on drugs? You won't be there to make those decisions for her. But you're here now to teach her how and to give her experience. That isn't going to happen if it's always Daddy to the rescue or Daddy barring the door.

We're not talking about the obvious. Of course you don't want her to watch R-rated movies or listen to music filled with sex and violence. You're careful about whose house she goes to to play, and you never leave her out in public alone. But when it comes to decision-making and problem-solving, too much protection can be stifling. We have a few suggestions for those of you who tend to go that way.

Find out why certain things scare you for her. Are you afraid of the image she's creating for herself? Afraid some sixth grade guy will take advantage of her? Afraid people will think you're a bad parent if she makes a mistake? Try to get that worked out in yourself, because as long as you're afraid, you'll want to control her every move.

Give her some guidelines and tools for making decisions and solving problems, things that work for you. If you're worried about particular things, go straight there. For example, if you're concerned about the sexualization of the culture and that's why you don't want her to give boys a thought or ever watch a television program, look at magazines with her and watch movies together and talk about occurrences you both witness in everyday life. Be in it together.

Let her make choices that won't have drastic results if she makes the wrong one. You can decide what the limits are within which she can experiment and explore. Point out her options and help her see the pros and cons, but don't always tell her what to do.

Give her some credit for being able to figure out how to solve problems. Suggestions are fine, but in the words of Paul Plant, counselor for families in conflict, "Just remember whose problem it is."[15]

Be her safety net, ready to comfort if she comes home crying. Don't criticize her, and do resist the urge to say, "I told you so."

Show her the people she can depend on for support as she navigates her way through the world. That would be God. Herself. You and her mother.

Let pain be a tool for learning. It's okay for her to be disappointed as long as you help her see what she now knows that she didn't know before.

If she tends to be irresponsible, and you don't think you can let her make decisions for herself, look at how often you are responsible *for* her. Do you micromanage her? Stand over her while she's doing her homework to make sure it gets done? Monitor her chores like the Gestapo? Fail to follow through when you've told her there will be consequences for not carrying out those responsibilities?

Hand the problem back to her. Ask her how she can structure her time or remember to get her work done. Take away privileges when she doesn't do what she's supposed to do. Then reward her for going above and beyond the basics. She'll test you—probably more than once—but be consistent.

As a single dad of two daughters, author and blogger Joe Kelly says don't pretend you can fix anything and everything or that you still know all, the way she thought you did when she was a sweet baby girlfriend. In the first place, she's aware that you can't and don't. If you keep telling her you have all the answers, she'll eventually become disillusioned with you, because you can't possibly live up to what you're still claiming you can do.

Talk to her about those areas where you can't totally protect and save her. As Joe Kelly says, "Show her your love is more important than your ability as Mr. Fix-It."[16]

———

My dad is really awesome, and our relationship has turned from a daddy-daughter thing to us being really good friends. I think it's helped with us being open with each other about things like growing up, and spending time with each other as much as we did when I was little.

— Age 16

It's going to scare you spitless — there's no question about that. But she'll gain the self-confidence you want her to have, and you'll be protecting her from making a mess of things when the stakes are higher.

What we're about here is getting you and your daughter to the place that at age sixteen, she'll say something like that about you. It isn't our aim to make you the perfect father. That guy doesn't exist. You're going to make small mistakes — it's inevitable. We're just going to help you get the big things right.

As our tween-dad friend Terry Esau says, hang on. The ride gets bumpier every day, and the bumps get bigger. You've gone from the kiddie roller coaster to the Top Thrill Dragster. "Your one-year-old learns to say, 'Uh-oh.' When she's eighteen, you could be the one saying, 'Uh-oh.'"[17] We know you'd rather be the one saying, "You're turning out great."

We're going to do all we can to help you get there.

2

What Happened to My Little Girl?

What Just Happened?

You sink into the Dad-Only chair and take a minute to soak in the silence of a Saturday afternoon. You've done everything on the honey-do list and picked up your kids from their respective soccer practices. Your wife's out shopping and your son and daughter are occupied somewhere else in the house. These tween years are great—you don't have to watch them every second to make sure they don't put your wallet down the garbage disposal or eat household cleanser. Nice.

You're just about to reach for the remote and see what's on ESPN when an ungodly shriek pierces through the air from the kitchen. Either there's a coyote loose in there or someone's been stabbed. You start to leap from the chair, but there's no need because your tween daughter is already standing in front of you, cheeks purple and eyes bulging like she has a serious thyroid condition. Most prominent is the object she's waving in your face while she continues to scream:

"He put it in the freezer, Dad! The *freezer*!"

"What is it?" you ask as something white and stiff continues to swing at you.

The conversation goes downhill from there.

"It's my bra!"

"Your *bra*?"

"*Yes!*"

"Since when do you wear a bra?"

"Da-ad, he put it in the freezer and now I can't wear it!"

"Who's 'he'?"

My dad doesn't seem to like me growing up. He says stuff like "What happened to the sweet little girl I used to have?"

You know, of course, but you're still trying to figure out why she needs a bra. She spews out her brother's name like a snake releasing venom.

"Are you sure it was him?" you say.

"He's the only one around here who's evil in his soul!"

So far she's said nothing that hasn't ended with an exclamation point. Time to defuse this situation.

"Where's your mother?" you say.

The protruding eyes now roll. "*You* told me she went shopping!"

"Well, when she gets home —"

"Why can't *you* do something?"

"You want me to kill your brother?"

"Yes."

That seems to calm her somewhat, but there's still the question of the stiff piece of white lingerie. She stops waving it and holds it out for your inspection. It looks more like a Band-Aid with a bow than any bra you've ever seen, and you've definitely never witnessed one with frost clustered around the hooks. You feel your lips twitch.

"This isn't funny, Dad!"

"No —"

"Then why are you laughing?"

"Honey, I'm not laughing," you say. Gurgle, actually.

"Yes, you are! You don't under*stand!*" She turns, frostbitten undergarment in hand, and storms toward her room. Over her shoulder she hurls her parting shot: "I hate all boys!"

You're fairly certain that includes you.

Out of the Mouths of Mini-Women

As a teen, I wish my dad had been able to relate to the physical and emotional changes I was going through in my tween years — and am still going through. Mom is great for that sort of stuff, but it's hard leaving one parent out and feeling awkward about it.

Here's the Deal

You've obviously had a relationship with a woman or, uh, you wouldn't be a father. You know about periods and bras and PMS and leg and armpit shaving. But it probably never hit you that it would all happen to your little girl when her hormones kicked in. Maybe it occurred to you in some vague, her-mother-will-take-care-of-that-stuff kind of way, but seriously? Single dads raising daughters are the exception, but for the most part, tween girls hear about menstruation and breast development and all the other manifestations of puberty from their moms, so dads don't worry about it too much.

But that doesn't mean you don't have a responsibility to know what's going on with your daughter's body. She is, as we've said, experiencing more physical changes between the ages of eight and twelve than at any other time in her life except for year one. If you think you're confused by the things you *can* see—little pre-breasts, hairier legs, the beginnings of curves, pimples dotting her forehead—think how bewildered she probably is by that *and* the things you *can't* see. So, yeah, in the midst of the what-is-happening-to-me angst, she needs a ton of support. Which means you need to get the necessary information so you'll feel comfortable and be accessible—should her brother put her 32A in the freezer or you are called on to run out for feminine hygiene products.

Here, in brief, is what you can expect in your daughter's tween years.

Puberty begins anywhere between the age of nine and thirteen these days. Younger than you thought, probably. That means breast buds, more hair on legs (and pits), a thicker waist, and wider hips. You might see a growth spurt, even in her face and definitely in her feet. Don't be surprised if you're footing the bill for new shoes every couple of months.

That often seems to happen literally overnight. One day she can still curl up in your lap—the next her legs are dangling over the side.

All that sudden growth means she may go through a klutzy stage while her brain figures out what to do with those extra inches in length. Five-point landings in the middle of the kitchen floor are not unheard of. She may go through a period when her athletic ability wobbles. She might even no longer be suited for a sport she's loved—gymnastics and dance being the two most obvious. On the other hand, she may suddenly be a natural for basketball or volleyball.

While she's looking more like a woman—or some facsimile thereof—she may act more like a small child at times. If she's scared by the stranger she now sees when she looks at her body, or she's getting peer pressure to be sophisticated when she's still into Webkins, or it's dawned on her that she's starting to separate from you and Mom—she's bound to experience some sleep problems, maybe a little separation anxiety, a lot of unexplained tears. We'll talk more about this in the next chapter, but just keep in mind for now that the hormones that are wreaking havoc (or will soon) affect her emotions as much as they do her physical self.

―――――――

I told my mom my jeans were too tight. My dad said maybe I shouldn't eat so much. My mom told me later when I was crying that I was just going through a growth spurt, but I'm sure my dad just thinks I'm fat. Maybe I am.

As if the normal changes of preadolescence weren't enough, your daughter is also vulnerable to society's general view of the female body. She's seeing print and broadcast ads where every desirable woman is stick-figure thin, blonde, and endowed with a C cup—traits obviously necessary for selling motorcycles, yogurt, and pain relievers. Movies and TV shows, including the animated variety, depict wasp-waisted women wielding weapons or corporate power while showing cleavage that rivals the Grand Canyon. There is pressure everywhere for women to be sexy, to be physically perfect, and to deny themselves basic nutrition to stay that way. When you get right down to it, about 2 percent of the female population actually looks like that, and even those are liberally Photoshopped.

All of that's coming down on your impressionable ten-year-old who has either no bra in her immediate future or feels like a heifer because she's filling out before she makes that growth spurt upward. It doesn't help that the boys her age are experiencing their own awkward puberty—which means they're likely to blurt out whatever comes to mind to cover their embarrassment when they realize the girls are getting breasts and waists and hips. And that they kind of like it.

Every bit of that is affecting your daughter's attitude toward her body and her relationship with food. Every bit of that—and you. Even if you never say anything to your tween girl about her weight or her height or her shape, that's a statement in itself. ("I must not even be worth noticing.") What you *do* say can make the difference between a healthy body image and a lifelong battle to be like the emaciated models being paraded before her. Do you really want her fighting a war she can never win—and shouldn't have to?

Your actions speak as loudly as your words. Stuff you might not even have thought about:

If and how you respect her privacy.

How you respond to the demeaning of women's bodies in the media.

How you handle her brothers' teasing.

The way you treat your wife physically.

Your own fitness.

You don't think she's paying attention to all that?

This whole body thing is huge for women. (Like you haven't picked up on that.)

It's hard, though, for guys to remember the huge difference between boys and girls when it comes to their physical selves. While for boys it's more important to *act* a certain way, for girls it's far more important to *look* a certain way. Ask any guy who's fifteen pounds overweight how he feels about himself and he'll probably say, "I'm good." Ask any woman who could stand to lose maybe ten and she'll say, "If I could just take off twenty-five pounds I'd be happy." I wouldn't advise actually asking her, however. Purely hypothetical.

In Reality

If you want to get a handle on where you are in this area, mark the statements that are NOT true for you.[1]

- ○ I resist the urge to comment on women's weight.
- ○ When my guy friends and work colleagues disrespect women, I call them on it.
- ○ I'm conscious of my own biases toward overweight people and work on those.
- ○ I tell my daughter what I value *in* her — her character, her personality, her abilities.
- ○ I talk to my daughter about unrealistic female images when we see them on TV, in movies, on billboards.
- ○ I refuse to keep anything around that objectifies women, like the *Sports Illustrated* swimsuit issue.
- ○ I set limits on the TV my daughter watches alone and on the sites she visits on the Internet.

My dad says things about how his big girl is growing up on him, but in a really loving way. I think he's proud that I'm growing up.

I wish my dad would understand that I need more privacy. Me and my brother share a room, so sometimes my dad and brother barge in without knocking. Even if the door is closed. Sometimes it seems like the only privacy I have is in the bathroom.

I can talk to my dad about everything. Well … almost everything. I can talk about everything with my mom but some things — you know, those things, I can't talk about with my dad. It would be way too embarrassing.

○ I teach my sons to be sensitive to and respectful of women, including their mother.

○ (For single dads raising daughters alone) I make sure she has positive female role models in her life.

○ I do physical recreational activities with my daughter.

○ I'm not into women being ultra-thin.

The ones you marked are the ones you'll want to pay special attention to in this chapter. The ones that *are* true for you? You're doing all right there, Dad, but read on anyway. You can't know too much when it comes to your daughter. Let's start with the ultimate parent.

Learning from the Master

When a woman has her regular flow of blood, the impurity of her monthly period will last seven days, and anyone who touches her will be unclean till evening.

Anything she lies on during her period will be unclean, and anything she sits on will be unclean. Whoever touches her bed must wash his clothes and bathe with water, and he will be unclean till evening. Whoever touches anything she sits on must wash his clothes and bathe with water, and he will be unclean till evening. Whether it is the bed or anything she was sitting on, when anyone touches it, he will be unclean till evening.

Leviticus 15:19–23

Wait. We're kidding, right? We're not seriously expecting you to …

Not even close. We offer this passage of Scripture as the sum total of what the Bible says about anything even remotely connected with puberty. We're not even going to think about what that was actually about, much less what, if anything, it means to us today. We'll just say that adhering to this commandment would mean a serious amount of laundry.

The point is, you're not going to get a whole lot of direct help from the sacred text in dealing with the physical changes in your tween daughter's body. But we *can* take our cue from something Paul wrote in his letter to the Colossians (3:21): "Fathers, do not embitter your children, or they will become discouraged."

It comes right after, "Children, obey your parents in everything, for this pleases the Lord." Want to insure that that happens? Then don't come down so hard on them, Paul says, that they figure it's not worth the effort to try to be anything but the hopeless scum you've made them think they are. For a guy who never had any kids, Paul nails it.

You want your daughter to be comfortable in her own skin? Not expose cleavage and navel and buns to the world at large? Be healthy? Know that she's worthy of respect as a woman?

None of that is going to happen if as a child she's been made to feel like she's fat, unattractive, and unlovable. It's going to be close to impossible if she's been given no defense against teasing and the sexualizing of her generation. Basically, there's no way she's going to have any decent, realistic view of herself as a female if you do any of the following. No way. As in nada.

Don't Say It, Dude ...

"You're putting on a little weight, aren't you sweetie?"

"No candy for you till you get rid of some of that baby fat."

"Why do you need your door closed? You got something to hide in there?"

"What do you need a bra for?"

"No daughter of mine's going out of here looking like a tramp."

"Take it easy, Klutz."

"This whole cramps thing is in your head. You're wimping out on me here."

"Your brother said the breast fairy passed you over? Just ignore him."

"You're too heavy to sit in my lap."

Your daughter's going to be, as Paul puts it, "discouraged" from time to time by other influences you can't control—much as you'd like to. You *can* control what happens at home, though, so do it. We're just about to show you how.

Where Do I Come In?

As we've said above, the issues like "Here's what's going to happen when you get your period" logically come under Mom's job description. Unless you have a very unusual situation at your house, you won't be the one going bra shopping with your tween or teaching her how to shave her legs even if she *does* use your razor to do it. There are, however, several areas where your input is vital. Some of them may surprise you.

Puberty. Find out from her mom where your daughter is in terms of her period and the other changes that are happening. You need to be approachable and unembarrassed by any of it (or at least appear to be). Be the dad she can come to if her period starts when Mom's not home or some boy snaps her bra at school or some Really Mean Girl calls her a cow. Be that man, that friend.

Eating Habits. Even if you aren't the one cooking or doing the grocery shopping for your family (although did you know that according to a 2008 study, 24 percent of the males surveyed said they were?),[2] you still have a major influence on your daughter's eating habits and nutrition, and that influence comes through example. The chef in the house (a.k.a. Mom) can put a healthy, well-balanced meal on the table and give a ten-minute exegesis on what it's going to do for everybody's bodies, but if you turn your nose up at it, she might as well have saved herself the effort. When a kid is already suspicious of anything green on the plate, your giving it the evil eye is all she needs to convince her it's poison. In other words, man up and eat your fruits and veggies and lay off the fat and sugar overload, because your daughter is watching. A few other things you can do to promote healthy eating (which, as you will note, do not include "You're going to sit there until that plate is clean."):

Praise the cooking and eat it like you enjoy it, says David Grotto, president of Nutrition Housecall.[3] Save any complaints about the tuna casserole for a private conversation.

Out of the Mouths of

Mini-Women

I think my dad loves me whoever I am. But I think he misses when I was little and carefree. Now that my body is getting ready to form into a woman, I think that's hard for him.

Model eating slowly, even if you tend to be a wolfer. Chew every mouthful until it's the consistency of applesauce. Seriously.

Don't stuff yourself, no matter how good it is. Eat until you're just full.

Don't let Mom be the nutrition Nazi. Back her up on her attempts to make healthy eating a habit. If that's not her MO, talk to her about teaming up on it.

If you have to cook for your daughter and you're hopeless in the kitchen (and we're not implying that you are, but just in case), pass up the prepared foods (frozen dinners, canned entrees, mac and cheese in a box) and go for the basics — fruit, raw veggies, cheese, hearty toast with natural peanut butter. Make sure she gets regular protein and that her snacks are low in sugar.

Strike the right balance between being a control freak and letting her run amuck. We don't know who thought to even run a study like this, but the results are scientific. In a 2006 study on obesity, it was determined that women who had highly controlling fathers had a higher percentage of body fat. A 2007 Australian study revealed that fathers who placed *no* limits on their children or weren't involved in their upbringing also were more likely to have overweight children than fathers who were present and placed sane limits on their children.[4]

Outlaw "diets" for your daughters (and discourage your wife from them too). At the first mention of going on the cabbage diet or the grapefruit diet or the SlimFast Plan, have a sit-down about the outright stupidity of fad diets *and* the ridiculousness of her worrying about being too fat at age nine. Even if your child is overweight, work with her mom — and a nutritionist if necessary — to change her eating habits, but don't refer to it as "putting her on a diet." Diets don't work. Good nutrition does.

Be alert for signs of eating disorders. Alert, not hypervigilant. You don't have to call a therapist every time her appetite slips a notch. Just know the symptoms so you'll recognize them if they show up. In a tween, that could be a refusal to eat, or a prolonged decline in appetite unrelated to any physical cause, or reports from the school that she's throwing away her lunch. According to Houston psychotherapist Mary Jo Rapini, there is a correlation between the relationships girls have with their fathers and their likelihood of developing an eating disorder.[5] Girls are less prone when their dads participate with them in healthy family activities, are open with their love, and support healthy eating. Those whose dads focus on their appearance, or ignore it all together, and who have none of the above positives from their fathers run a greater risk.

Remember that this is as good for you as it is for your growing daughter. You do want to live to walk her down the aisle, yeah?

Sack Time. A tween girl needs between nine and ten hours of sleep a night. Period. As she creeps toward adolescence — or even before if she's anxious or off-the-wall energetic — she may have trouble falling asleep at bedtime, but enforce her being in bed at a set time anyway. Encourage her to have a cool-down time before she hops in, and be a part of that. Don't think she's too old to be read to or too young to pray with you. Ten minutes of quiet talk can not only nudge her toward sleep but it can give you a peek into what's going on in her life. Marijean — a longer-than-you-could-listen-to-her talker anyway — was her most forthcoming when she was tucked in, including everything evil anybody said to her during the day and everything evil she said back to them. We never wanted her to go to sleep with all of *that* still running around in her brain.

Off the Couch. As much moving around as tween girls do, you wouldn't think getting enough exercise would be an issue. But according to a 2000 study of American children between six and twelve, the average time spent outdoors in unstructured play per week was thirty minutes.[6] Experts say that the lack of an adequate amount of exercise children used to get naturally from playing is a major reason why obesity in children has increased by four times over the past forty years,[7] putting them at risk for Type 2 diabetes, high blood pressure, and high cholesterol, even as children. If that isn't enough for you, this might be: child therapists Elium and Elium say that physically active girls are less likely to get pregnant, drop out of school, or put up with abuse.[8] You don't have her off the couch yet?

Some suggestions:

Be active with her. That goes beyond dropping her off at soccer practice. Ride bikes together. Go swimming. Take hikes. Shoot baskets. Do forward rolls across the backyard. Make it a family thing if you can.

Be supportive of any physical activity she wants to do, including a sport you know she's not going to star in. Does it really matter if she's the shortest girl in her class and she still wants to play basketball? Does it seriously make a difference that she wants to be on the soccer team because all her friends are? Why is that a problem, as long as she's active and having fun? She doesn't have to be great. She doesn't even have to be a little bit good. She just has to enjoy it.

If she is good at a sport, keep these things in mind:

- Young female athletes — especially those ages eleven and twelve — have special needs because their bodies are growing, and they require different coaching and conditioning than more mature athletes. Make sure her coach knows that.
- Tween girls who take up a sport early on and play that, and only that, year round in their elementary and middle school years can be at risk for serious injuries. Make sure there's a break in her sports schedule.
- Early specialization can actually prevent her from developing overall balance and strength and well-rounded coordination, which also makes her susceptible to injury. Make sure she plays more than one sport.

If your daughter tries a sport and it doesn't work out for her, and she thereafter goes into a fetal position every time you utter the word *athletic*, do a little gentle investigating. I didn't do that with Marijean, and as a result, in my opinion, she was robbed of some great experiences.

A babysitter we had when she was four suggested we put her in a gymnastics class with the babysitter's little boy. At first Marijean was excited, wanted to sleep in her pink leotard, the whole thing. Then one day, she had a meltdown going into the gym, which led to some questioning on the babysitter's part, revealing that Marijean had been "uncooperative" during her previous session and was given a reprimand and a time-out. Essentially she was busted. Her offense: refusing to try hard enough. So much for gymnastics — her choice as well as ours.

Unfortunately, after that — especially in her tween years — anytime we mentioned lessons or teams, forget about it. Nancy didn't go out of her way to encourage Marijean because she had some bad experiences in things athletic when she was a kid that sapped any confidence she needed to enjoy even a bike ride. I kick myself now because Marijean has an athletic body, she's coordinated, and she likes to be active. If I had stepped in and given her some positive reinforcement, she could've enjoyed team sports and had a better body image. Once I started doing some things with her—snow skiing, rock climbing—and saw what a natural she was, I was even more upset with myself for not encouraging her sooner. Don't make that same mistake. If your daughter has a gag reflex about athletics, it's worth some looking into.

Sports aren't the only form of exercise—an important thing to remember if your daughter isn't an athlete. Dance, cheerleading, horseback riding, and skating all provide the same physical benefits as being on an organized team. Don't tease her about those being girly activities. Uh, she's a girl. And if there's a tournament or recital, be there. Video camera in hand.

Make sure she has time for free play. It isn't only the TV and the computer that have made just running around with friends almost obsolete. It's the fear that if you let her out the back door to climb trees or do cartwheels with her BFFs, someone's going to come along and snatch her. There's a huge difference between sending her down to the park at dusk for a game of unsupervised pickup soccer and keeping an eye on her and her girl buds while they play a round of shrieking tag on the front lawn. Not only is unstructured run-around time good for her physically, it exercises her imagination. Making up games and trying on roles are as important as building muscle and developing coordination. If your daughter isn't interested in organized sports, it's even more important for her to just ... move. Regularly.

Don't Say It, Dude ...

"You don't keep your eye on the ball out there. You've got to be
   more heads-up."

"I can see what you're doing wrong and you can't, so let me just
   tell you ..."

"If you're not going to take your sport seriously, I don't see why you even bother to play."

"We're going to work on your free throws at home. You're embarrassing yourself."

"I don't yell that much during your games."

"Your game was way off today."

"You have to stick with this so you can get a college scholarship."

Who She Thinks She Is. I know it seems freaky to think that before she even gets her own breasts, she's influenced by the ones being touted as the ones to have. But as we've pointed out, our daughters are inundated with images that tell them what their bodies are supposed to look like. And when they don't look like that—and 98 percent of the time they *don't*—their idea of themselves is twisted into something they may struggle with the rest of their lives. You can do a lot to make sure your daughter doesn't go there, that she is comfortable in her own skin.

Share this fact with Mom if she needs to hear it: Tweens and young teen girls' body image is impacted more by the negative attitude and comments of their mothers than by anything else.[9] Even remarks like "You've got grandma's thighs—you're never going to be able to wear a mini-skirt," can make her think she's about as attractive as a fire hydrant.

Talk to your daughter's mom about the way she refers to her own body. She can tell your daughter daily—hourly—what a cute little body she has—but that's yada-yada-yada compared to what she says about herself. "I'm so fat," "I need to lose about fifteen pounds," "I like her outfit, but I'd look like a cow in it." It's important for every mother to stifle that kind of talk around her daughter, but it's huge for moms who would shrivel up and die if they lost fifteen pounds. A girl going through a prepubescent chubby phase hears that and thinks, "If *she's* fat, then I must be a blimp."

Trust me. That happened in our house. During Marijean's tween years, Nancy was borderline anorexic and agonized over every ounce that came and went. Marijean, a robust, perfectly proportioned kid, grew up thinking she had to be a rail and knew she was never going to be. We've all tasted the regret and worked it through, but my wife and my daughter still have to hold each other to the "no I'm-so-fat rule."

Don't let her buy into the media image thing. Every time you see it, every time you hear it, turn to your daughter and tell her it's baloney. Every time. Educate her about air brushing and Photoshopping. Talk about what models have to do to get their hip bones to stick out like that. Tell her you think they look half-starved to you. Just don't let her buy in to it. And by all means, don't avoid the word *sexy*, because even at ten, eleven, and twelve, she's getting the message that that's what she has to be. Watched a set of tweenage cheerleaders perform lately? There's as much bumping and grinding as you'll find on any given night in Las Vegas. Let her know that no girl her age should be or can be sexy, and that no girl at any age should actually go for that look in an attempt to be loved. If it's not too soon for her to have gotten the concept of "sexy," it's not too soon for you to talk about it. And no, "go ask your mother" is not an option here. She needs to hear it from you.

On the other hand, don't assume she's being "sexual" if she runs from the bathroom to her room in a towel and stops at three other places in the house along the way. In her mind she's still a little girl. Be impressed that she knows enough not to streak naked down the hall, and for Pete's sake, don't shame her. As blogger Shanna Jayson put it, "Their bodies are maturing faster than their view of themselves as women."[10] And don't be too bewildered if the next minute she closes and locks her door and demands "some privacy around here!" She does need privacy. You can encourage her to be modest by letting her have it. And by explaining to her when she wants to wear a bikini on a family beach outing that this would be a great time to start respecting her body by not sharing every detail of it with the world. Again, don't accuse her of wanting to be sexual. It probably hasn't occurred to her that people are going to react differently to her blossoming body than they did to her little-girl, pot-bellied, flat-chested one. We discourage you from saying, "Adult men are going to be looking at you — you've got to cover up." That just sets her up to think she's always in danger from men. Focus on self-respect — and do that by, obviously, respecting her. If she does say she wants to look sexy, take a deep breath before you light into her or break out the chastity belt. Ask her what exactly "looking sexy" means to her, and you'll probably get a whole different definition than the one you have in mind.

Be more about the amazing things her body can do than about how it looks, no matter how cute it is. Praise her for trying physical skills. Celebrate with her when she can reach higher, run farther, or outmaneuver her big brother better than she did last year. Talk about how great you both feel after a hike or a swim or a bike ride. Even if your daughter couldn't pitch a ball or tap dance if her BFF depended on it, she can still feel good about what her body can do and know how cool it is to be healthy.

If your daughter is overweight or even just putting on pounds for that next increase in height, don't tell her that outright. Don't. No matter how cool you are when you say it or how big a smile you wear or how much you tell her *you* think she's beautiful just the way she is, the *but* is there, and it can be devastating. She's already insecure about the way her body's shaping up at this point, and those few words can chisel away at her view of herself. Just work with her mom on improving her diet and getting more physical activity into her life—and make that applicable to the whole family without singling her out. She doesn't need her brother saying, "If you weren't so fat, we could have dessert again. Nice goin'."

Boy Teasing. You're going to hear the refrain "I HATE boys!" more than once during her tween years. Those may in fact be your three favorite words strung together, since that means she hasn't picked up on their charms yet—quite frankly because they don't have any at this point. Their MO is more about teasing her until she's hitting, crying, or shrieking—or all of the above. Hence the "I HATE boys!" You know—having been an absurd little creep yourself once—that they're doing it to get her attention and propel themselves to the top of the social ladder, and because they're both attracted to and terrified by the changes that are happening in her (i.e., she is no longer just a soft boy). *She* doesn't know that, nor does she care. She just wants them to stop, and with good reason. Boys aren't dipping pigtails into inkwells anymore (what the heck's an inkwell?) or merely accusing their female counterparts of having "cooties" (nobody knows what they are either). Because they're exposed to more sex-laden TV shows, sarcastic radio

DJs, and blatantly raunchy music lyrics than tween boys have ever been, they have more teasing material than you did at that age, and they're using it, even when they don't exactly know what it means. Hey, anything for a laugh from their homies. What to do if she's really having a hard time with the ALCs (Absurd Little Creeps, a.k.a. boys)?

Tell her to ignore their comments. They get bored easily and move on when they don't get the reaction they want.

Let her know this is one instance when that eye-rolling she's so good at is totally appropriate. It's so wonderfully dismissive, and even the densest boy-kid won't miss it.

Encourage her to tell you if the teasing gets really ugly and/or sexual or if there's touching involved. She might hate the idea of tattling, but explain that tattling is done to get somebody *in* trouble and telling is done to get somebody *out* of trouble—her! She needs to know early on that sexual harassment is not okay and that she should always, always do something about it. Not a good time for you to threaten to beat the doo-doo out of the kid, however. She'll come to you again next time if you handle the situation with integrity this time.

If the teasing is coming from her brothers, put the kibosh on it immediately. There's a difference between family jokes that are fun for everybody and personal attacks that hurt *anybody.* Don't tell her she's overly sensitive, that that's the way boys are, that she should tease Billy back. Tell Billy to knock it off. Then don't let *her* get away with teasing *him,* and don't model teasing yourself. Why should anybody have to develop a thick skin to being taunted? It's the taunter who's wrong, not the tauntee. Teach that lesson at home, and your son won't be making some other tweenie miserable in public.

What About Affection? One of the worst tragedies of the increase in reported cases of sexual abuse in families is the effect it's had on good fathers who are sickened at the thought. It's actually painful to hear the dad of a tween girl say he's afraid to touch his daughter because somebody might think he's a pervert.

What?

At the time when she needs reassurance the most, when she needs to know she's loved no matter how funky she feels about herself and the changes that are happening to her—that is the all-time *worst*

Out of the Mouths of

Mini-Women

Since I'm getting older and my body is changing, it makes our relationship awkward, but we like to laugh together a lot.

moment to decide to withdraw all physical affection. It's hard to even know where to *start* naming the reasons why that isn't a good idea.

If she's starved for affection, she's going to fill up on something else—food, boys (there are boy-crazy ten-year-olds for a reason), the approval of the popular girls. Whatever it is, it isn't going to satisfy the reassurance she needs from your continued hugs and cheek kisses and snuggles while you watch a movie.

She needs to know it's okay to be touched in respectful, loving ways. It's a basic human need. Without it, we all get a little nutty.

This is a confusing time in so many ways. She needs the comfort and reassurance of your strong hand on her shoulder.

There's some grieving going on at times as she leaves her little girl-ness behind. Your scratchy whiskers on her cheek and the smell of your shirt as she buries her head in your chest remind her that she will always be your little girl.

So maintain the same kind of physical affection you've always given her. Just make sure it

comforts her.
affirms her.
supports her.
respects her boundaries.
helps her feel special.
is given with her spoken or tacit permission.

Isn't that what you've always done? Why stop now? DO NOT let the prevalence of sexual abuse keep you from showing your daughter that you love her.

Bridging the Gap

God, as the ultimate Father, you know I can't raise this daughter on my own, especially when it comes to her pubescent changes. Please bridge the major gap between what I know to do for her in this mind-boggling stage of her life and what she needs to grow into the woman you made her to be. Can't do it alone. Counting on you, Father.
Amen.

3

She'll Be Crying in a Minute

What Just Happened?

You're at the dinner table, saying pretty much the same things you've said every night since the kids were in high chairs.

"How was everybody's day?"

"Hey, you, Shorty—use a napkin, please."

"Could somebody hand me the ketchup? No, don't go out for a long pass—just give it to your sister and she can give it to me."

"So, kiddo, did you ace that math test or what?"

You receive the same nods and grins and open-mouthed chewing you always do as well as the occasional eye roll, a new addition to the supper fare. Basically, all is well at the king's banquet table.

And then suddenly your tween daughter starts to giggle. It's a small, throaty sound at first, bubbling up from a place deep in her girl-child soul where something you said struck the hysterics reflex.

The laughter morphs into full-blown guffaws. Her hands go over her mouth to avoid the spewing of food, and her eyes bulge. While she clutches her sides and tilts leeward in the chair, you blink at your wife. Her face remains impassive except for the eyebrow lifted in a "What?"

"What?" The kid's about to choke on her mashed potatoes for no apparent reason and her mother's saying, "What?"

Meanwhile, the lips that were seconds ago helpless with hilarity have begun to twist, and the eyes are brimming. Whatever was roll-on-the-floor funny has turned tragic.

"Do you see this?" you say to her mother. "She'll be crying in a minute."

Out of the Mouths of Mini-Women

I wish my dad understood how hard it can be growing up. I don't think he gets all the changes that are happening. Especially the emotional ones.

Too late. She already is. So hard that she jerks from the chair, hand·still smothering her mouth, and leaves the table to run down the hall. Her sobs are audible even after she slams her bedroom door. You stare once more at your wife.

"What just happened?" you say.

"She's an eleven-year-old girl," she says.

"What's that got to do with it?"

"Everything," she says.

And you are left completely and thoroughly clueless.

Out of the Mouths of Mini-Women

Sometimes I feel like I'm really mad for nothing, and I become extremely irritable at the SLIGHTEST thing. It comes in phases, where things seem louder than they normally do, when silly little things get on my nerves extremely. I suppose this is normal for our age, but it can be so annoying.

Here's the Deal

I can't even tell you how many times that scene was replayed at our dinner table. In our car. In the middle of Costco. I never did find out what went down or what I said to get that roller coaster of emotions careening up the track. Not even once. Probably didn't need to because Nancy was right: Marijean was just being an eleven-year-old girl.

Before you start thinking, "Oh, so we can chalk it all up to hormones," let me stop you, lest you make the mistake of actually saying that to your daughter. You thought she was freaking out before — just mention that she's got pubescent PMS and see what happens. Whether your tween daughter's mood swings are off the chart or mere blips on the screen, her emotions at this age are way more complicated than her estrogen. It's a good idea to understand where they're coming from or you're going to spend a lot of time not only feeling clueless but saying all the things that are guaranteed to run that roller coaster right off into midair.

The good news is, you can actually do a lot to make this up-and-down time easier for your daughter (not to mention you). It starts with having a clear picture of all the things that are going on in her ever-changing self. To make it as simple as possible, we've narrowed it down to four parts.

The part that's just a matter of being female. You don't have to be a psychologist to notice that there are clear differences in the way men and women think and feel. Your daughter's a mini-woman, so why shouldn't that apply to her?

Girls are more sensitive to your body language than boys. If you have a son, you know you can stand there glaring at him for a full two minutes before he stops what he's doing and says, "Huh?" He's not stupid—he's just a boy. Girls, on the other hand, tend to pick up every nuance. You twitch your lips and your daughter knows you're laughing at her on the inside. You blink more than twice and she nails you for not understanding her. Even if she doesn't say it, your tween daughter knows the tightening of your jaw muscles means you're losing patience and the glances darting over her head mean you're losing interest. Give it up, guy. You can't hide anything.

Girls are in tune with how people relate to each other and to them. If you and your wife are having momentary issues, your tween daughter knows it the minute she walks in the house. Forget about concealing from her that your brother-in-law is getting on your nerves. She can tell who thinks she's adorable and who wishes she'd go play somewhere else. How does she do that? Her brain is wired to receive and decipher enormous amounts of sensory information,[1] which means she can pick up on unsaid conversations (the kind husbands and wives have with each other), subtexts, and things-between-the-lines, all of which most of us guys miss entirely. In other words, she knows what's really going on, and it can send her into a tailspin that is inexplicable to you.

As for the things they actually hear, *girls use more parts of their brains when they're listening than men do.*[2] They're also more naturally skilled at noticing changes in tone of voice. That means your daughter makes a lot of connections while you're talking and attaches meanings to all of them. Bottom line: she gets messages you didn't know you sent, and probably didn't mean to. That explains why she can storm off after a two-line conversation while you stand there thinking, *What? What did I say?*

Girls notice things in greater detail and remember them longer.[3] Have you ever told a story about an event shared by the family without your daughter—or her mother—interrupting you to tell you that you have some inconsequential fact wrong? Hopefully you haven't tried to dispute it. Come on, you know she's probably right. It all goes into a vault in her brain and can be pulled out at the slightest

Out of the Mouths of Mini-Women

Sometimes my dad treats me like a baby. And sometimes he's AWESOME. But I never know which he'll be today.

provocation, which means she can become prickly all over again about something that set her off months ago.

The personal stuff of life is more significant to girls than it is to boys.[4] If you want proof, forget your anniversary. If your daughter's BFF blows her off, she can be distraught for days. That goes on all the time (as in hourly—see chapter 6), and her emotions go with it. For girls, it's almost always more about how it feels than what it means.

A girl sees the big picture.[5] And not just figuratively but physically. Girls and women actually have a wider peripheral vision because they have more receptor rods and cones in the retinas of the eyes.[6] And let's face it, what your daughter sees is not always pretty. If you picked up on all the subtleties and undercurrents and possibilities for disaster that she does, you'd be moody and dramatic and weepy too.

Probably most puzzling is the fact that although boys and girls experience the same emotions, *girls express their feelings more freely and more often.*[7] To you, she's overreacting. To her—she's just feeling what she thinks. According to Daniel Goleman, author of *Emotional Intelligence*, it takes the first twenty years of her life for her to discriminate between her thoughts and her feelings so her emotions don't tip that seesaw totally to one position or the other.[8] Hang in there. You only have another ten years to go.

Females use conversation differently than men. For them it's a way to be more intimate with people, to give and receive support, to get everybody on the same page. When they talk, they just want to connect. Males, on the other hand, use conversation to solve problems and give advice, not to mention show their superiority. So here comes your daughter, wanting to share her feelings with you, and you tell her how to solve the problem. She goes off crying and you wonder what just went down.

The part you CAN chalk up to hormones. We can't emphasize this too much: every mood swing your daughter has isn't automatically the result of a sudden surge of estrogen. But hormonal changes do play a part. As one blogger put it, "The hormones start to course through her body—and your house."[9] The good news is, the moods she can't seem to control because they're chemically induced are only temporary. Even though the changes continue with each menstrual

Out of the Mouths of

Mini-Women

I wish my dad understood that when I'm on my period it's harder for me to act and be a certain way. I know he knows about it but he doesn't get that sometimes I don't want to talk to anybody. If he could just not always ask me what's wrong or talk to me when I obviously don't want to be talked to, that would be wonderful.

cycle, they'll eventually affect her less dramatically. But you have to figure, she's got that whole period thing to deal with (which, I gotta tell you, makes me glad I'm a guy), the breasts appearing out of nowhere, the legs and armpits getting hairier and making her a prime target for teasing, the new odors to contend with—and she's painfully self-conscious about all of it. Plus, with the hormones comes a budding interest in boys, so she actually cares if they say she has man-legs or sniff like cartoon bloodhounds because she forgot to use her deodorant. She has a lot of fun stuff going on too—the girly things, the new opportunities in sports, all that—but there are bound to be moments when the cramps and the crushes and the furry armpits will reduce her to tears. It's hard for us to comprehend, but do yourself and her a favor and try. It might help you both to realize that she doesn't understand a lot of those ups and downs any more than you do.

If, by the way, you think your daughter seems less emotionally mature in her tween years than she was before, you're right. Those hormones are making her feel things more intensely, and it's hard for her to tame the unfamiliar emotions. It would be like your never having really been angry before in your life and suddenly discovering that everything—everything—is ticking you off and people are saying, "Man, you need to calm down. You're too old for this." You'd want to punch somebody's lights out. So does she, only she's more likely to cry, accuse you of *not* understanding her at *all*, slam her door, or hate herself. If not all of those. In no particular order.

The part that's trying to figure out who she is. Even if your daughter isn't ultra-sensitive to her hormones, she's still in her preadolescence, facing even more huge changes as she approaches thirteen. She's not consciously saying, "Yikes, I've got to get mentally ready for my teen years," but that's exactly what's happening. Those brooding hours in her room don't mean she's depressed, and the abrupt spurts of energy and optimism don't indicate that she's bipolar. She's just trying on selves, testing out behaviors, taking her new discoveries for a test drive.

As for the tears—they don't qualify her for drama queen. Sometimes she's just afraid she can't handle the world ahead. Dude, I feel

Out of the Mouths of Mini-Women

I wish my dad understood that when I have my door closed, it's not because I want to shut myself off and just be a loner. It's just that I want to be alone.

The thing I wish is — well, sometimes I don't want to be teased and sometimes there's nothing else I want to do but laugh. I wish my dad knew the difference.

like that myself sometimes. The thing is, you can't make all of that okay for her so she'll go back to her old self. That self is gone, and it's being replaced by a young woman. That can be harder if she was Daddy's little princess and you were the hero, the one who could do no wrong, and now you're getting "You just don't understand" as she stomps off in tears. Just remember, the mini-eruptions aren't really about you. They're about her trying to figure out who she is now that she knows you're fallible (as in, you don't get her any more than she gets herself).

A lot of this depends on her individual emotional style. Your daughter may be a holder-inner who broods and ponders in her room or in the back of the SUV. It's easy to mistake her sullen silences for rudeness (okay, sometimes that's what it is, but we'll get to that below) or decide she's pulling attitude, especially when those phases are punctuated with brighter, sunnier periods. All that inner turmoil can wear her out.

By contrast, your tween might be an exploder who shares every emotional thing with everybody. We sometimes had Mount Saint Marijean at our house where she just spewed everything that had been roiling inside her for a week. I'd think, "What's with the temper?" Like my sister said about her tween daughter, "My sweet baby child has turned into the Tasmanian Devil." All that outer turmoil can wear *you* out.

However she expresses it, she's struggling to become self-reliant. You want her to be, but ironically right now you represent everything that holds her back from the total independence she wants but isn't ready for. That would account for the withdrawal, the over-accusing, the overstating of your awfulness. Words like "you always" and "you never" are brandished like weapons. That doesn't mean you let her aim at you and fire—we'll talk about that later in the chapter. But just so you know, you're not a loser father and she's not a lost-cause daughter just because she loses it now and then.

The part that's testing you. Several times when Marijean was in her tweens, I got these flashbacks of her at about a year and a half, climbing up on the hearth and looking back over her shoulder to see if I was going to tell her to get down. It was the same thing as her pushing my limits at age nine. It was just cuter when she was in diapers.

Same deal though, really. Just like when she was a toddler, your daughter's at another place where she's getting a new sense of herself. Back then she found out she could toddle away from you and say "no." Now she can say more than "no." She may interpret your limits (as reasonable as they are) as "You don't trust me," "You think I'm a baby," "You don't believe in me."

That in itself is enough to deal with. Then there's the fact that, as we've pointed out, kids are being pressured by society to grow up too fast, and the transition from tween to teen is so short it's scary. Grammar school, for instance, used to last through the eighth grade, and then students went on to high school at age fourteen. Then we invented junior high school, which was seventh, eighth, and ninth grades, putting kids in high school at age fifteen. Even better. But then somebody came up with the bright idea of middle school, which starts in sixth grade, eleven-year-olds, and puts them in with seventh and eighth graders who are twelve, thirteen, and sometimes fourteen. You've got kids just starting puberty bumping into guys in the halls who have started to shave. They have to try to act somewhat sophisticated just to survive.

Not to mention their exposure to sex, drugs, and peer pressure before they even *get* to middle school, via the Internet, tween-targeted TV, and role models who border on skanky. How is a girl nine or ten years old supposed to find the core of herself when she thinks she has to emulate junior sex goddesses? There's going to be some angst involved.

There is so much change going on for her, she'll sometimes test to make sure *you* are the same. Are you still going to put her in her place if she back talks you? Are you going to continue to make sure she eats right and gets enough sleep? Do you care as much about her grades and her attitude and her sportsmanship as you always have? She's probably not going to just come right out and ask you. She's more likely to push you until you lower the boom. Even then she

I think my dad guesses the reason I'm always acting strange is because of hormones. But instead of helping me by talking through it when I don't know what I want, he just tells me I should "be mature for once" or yells at me. He doesn't understand my female brain and what I need. So I never trust him with my feelings.

may prance off pouting to her room, but she's relieved, an emotion you *won't* know about.

All of that is normal for a tween girl. Your challenge as the dad is (a) to understand what's going on and (b) to guide her through it. Neither of those things means you have to put up with disrespect and rudeness. Having compassion for what she's going through is one thing. Letting her turn into the Wicked Witch of the West is another. There are certain behaviors that, while they're common in tween girls, need to be corrected:

Out of the Mouths of

Mini-Women

My dad definitely lets me be myself, unless I think I'm "being myself" when I'm just doing something wrong.

Saying, "I hate you!" out loud.

Yelling, "Why can't you just leave me alone?"

Slamming the door in your face.

Muttering under her breath as she walks away from you.

Dismissing you with a "whatever," a "du-uh," or an eye roll that isn't done in fun (remember that dad who needed a guidebook for eye rolling?).

Being deliberately mean to her siblings.

Blatantly disregarding the house rules.

Those don't just come with the tween territory. And if they're administered by her as tests, you can't afford to fail or the next eight to ten years of your life—and perhaps beyond—are going to be your own personal hell. Not to mention hers.

Marijean never exhibited anything quite that in-your-face, but she did develop a serious 'tude when she was ten. Nancy and I were going through a rough time, and our daughter was obviously anxious and didn't know what to do with it. She showed me that by taking up with a neighborhood girl a couple of years older than she was and copying her lip curls and hair tosses and loaded sighs. I let it go. But the day they let themselves into our next door neighbor's house while they were away was the day I knew we were losing ground fast. I made it up in a hurry, but if I'd paid attention sooner to the hair-tossing and lip-curling, we could have avoided the breaking and entering. We did head off future problems by finally paying attention to the acting out and acting *on* it. Just saying—certain behaviors aren't the way anybody "just is," and you don't have to put up with them.

Learning from the Master

Most of us parents really dig this verse from Ephesians:

> *Children, do what your parents tell you. This is only right. "Honor your father and mother" is the first commandment that has a promise attached to it, namely, "so you will live well and have a long life."*
>
> Ephesians 6:1–3, *The Message*

Even those of us who aren't in the habit of throwing Scripture verses in our kids' faces are at least familiar with this one and nod enthusiastically when we hear it. "Do what your parents tell you." That's what I'm talkin' about.

But like most passages that we take out of context, this one has been subject to some serious misinterpretation. It's right up there with Ephesians 5:22: "Wives, submit to your husbands as to the Lord." Fathers/husbands in particular tend to stop there without reading on to the other half of that deal. "Husbands, love your wives, just as Christ loved the church and gave himself up for her" (verse 25). And, more to the point here: "Fathers, don't exasperate your children by coming down hard on them. Take them by the hand and lead them in the way of the Master" (6:4, *The Message*).

At least when your tween daughter is exasperated, you're going to know about it. Already loaded for bear with hormones, peer pressure, and societal expectations, any frustration with you, Dad, is going to be right out there for you to see. You're going to know without a doubt that you are not currently taking her by the hand and leading her in the way of the Master. No, you're driving her nuts.

So try to wrap your mind around this: if you want your daughter to do what you tell her to, if you expect her to honor you and her mom, if you want her to live well and have a long life (i.e., you want her to survive her childhood), your best bet is to learn the way of the Master and pass that on to her. Jesus wasn't an earthly parent, but he was here representing the Father in the following ways that you can emulate with your daughter:

A full understanding of who he was working with. This book, we hope, is a start. The rest comes with spending a lot of time with your girl. A lot of time.

I wish my dad would listen when I say, "Don't do anything today that would in the least bit bug me. Just don't." He always asks for a reason why and then he usually gets worse.

Honoring is hard work.

Compassion. There was no "I'm here to straighten you people out." It was all about "I know what you're struggling with and I'm going to love you through it."

Patience. To an appropriate point. All that "you brood of vipers" stuff was aimed at the Pharisees, which your daughter is not. When he did get testy with the disciples, it was because he'd done everything short of dying, and they still weren't getting it. But he went ahead and died for them anyway. That's patience.

Complete honesty. He told it like it was, though never in a critical, judgmental way (except in the case of the aforementioned Pharisees, whom your daughter bears no resemblance to whatsoever). People knew where they stood with him, and where they stood was in the light of his love.

Unconditional love. Even when he was saying, "Peter, you numbskull," there was never a doubt that he would lay down his life for his friends no matter what they did. He didn't pull punishing silences on them or indicate that they weren't worth his time, that he had more important things to do than reassure them. And any kid within a hundred-yard radius seemed to end up on his lap no matter what he was in the middle of.

You're not Jesus. But if you're even trying to model yourself after him, you aren't going to "exasperate" your daughter. If you need a little more elaboration on that, here we go.

In Reality

This is a quick check on the things you might be saying that are pushing your daughter's exasperation buttons. Mark any of these that come close to anything you've heard yourself say to the tween girl in your life:

- ○ "Hey, Monkey." (Stinker, Butterball, Pooh Bear, or any other nickname you called her back when she thought it was fun to be your monkey, stinker, butterball, or pooh bear.)
- ○ "Way to go, Klutz. Somebody just put that wall there."
- ○ "If those freckles ever grow together, you're going to have one great tan."

- ○ "Do you want some cheese with that whine?"
- ○ "Look out—here come the tears—guaranteed."
- ○ "What's that boat doing in the living room? Oh, wait, that's your shoe."
- ○ "Let me get my share of those mashed potatoes before [insert daughter's name] digs into them."
- ○ "You didn't *know* that? I thought everybody knew that."
- ○ "Keep talking. Just wake me up when you get to the point."
- ○ "You don't have to take everything so seriously. I was only kidding."
- ○ "If you can't learn to take a joke, you've got a rough road ahead of you, girl."

I know it's tempting to mash those buttons, especially when they're so clearly marked, but it's not worth it, trust me. Your daughter's sensitive to this stuff, and she's got enough to contend with when it comes from ALCs (Absurd Little Creeps, a.k.a. boys), RMGs (Really Mean Girls), and even her BFFs on a bad day. Be the one she can count on not to send her over the edge by avoiding the kinds of statements you marked above. And in general:

Look at why you're teasing her. Probably it's just because you're a guy and that's how guys show girls they're interested in them. You think you're showing affection and she thinks you're telling her she's clumsy and ugly and totally inept. Her brothers can tease her and she blows it off (hopefully). Boys at school poke at her and she rolls her eyes. You do it and she dissolves into a puddle. You're not a guy to her. You're Dad.

A little gentle teasing, the kind that actually makes her smile rather than implode, is fun. But if what you consider to be affectionate banter brings her to tears, it doesn't matter whether it's funny to you or not—you've struck a nerve. Basically, if it isn't fun for both of you, leave it alone.

Avoid teasing that points out she's inadequate in some area or doesn't know something that, for Pete's sake, why would she? If she's learning to water ski, don't poke fun at her because it took her fifteen tries to get up. If ballet didn't turn out to be her thing, don't nickname her Twinkle Toes. If she tried to make tuna salad and went a little

Out of the Mouths of Mini-Women

My dad does things that really annoy me, like messing with my hair when I'm really working hard on a project. He ruins my concentration, and I ask him to stop, but he purposely keeps on doing it just to annoy me. He thinks it's all in fun, but I'm serious because he's causing a problem. Then he says, "Why are you being so angry all the time?"

overboard with the mayo, don't start calling her Chef Clueless. You aren't "toughening her up" by making fun of her. You're just making her resentful. And who said she had to be tough anyway?

Don't tease her about anything she feels vulnerable about. If she's going through a chubby phase, or her breasts have blossomed over-night, or she struggles with anything remotely athletic, those subjects are strictly taboo. Don't worry that she "can't take a joke." Why is anybody required to "take a joke" that's insensitive? So she seems to be taking herself a little too seriously these days. When everything stops seeming so huge, she'll get past that. For now, leave her tender spots alone.

Always be ready to laugh **with** *her, but never* **at** *her.* Don't get too hung up on her being able to laugh at herself. Model laughing at *your*self and let her decide what's funny about *her*self. That's not pussy-footing around, walking on eggshells. It's just being consider-ate of her feelings. Again, your goal isn't to give her a thick skin. It's to allow her to feel comfortable in the skin she's in.

Never—and it's hard to do this—but never, ever make fun of her if she's crying because someone dies in a movie. It's real to her and it's a way for her to get out the stuff inside of her that she doesn't even understand. The tears mean she has feelings, that she isn't shallow.

If you mess it up, apologize. "I was only *kidding*!" doesn't qualify as an apology. When she falls apart because you've just pointed out that she's about as graceful as an eighteen-wheeler, explain to her why you say stuff like that. As one father tells his twelve-year-old stepdaughter, "I love. Therefore I tease." Tell her you can see that it hurts her feelings and that even though you didn't mean for it to, you're sorry. Ask her what would make a difference for her. No teasing at all? No teasing about certain subjects? No teasing in front of her friends? Make sure the agreement works both ways; if she's going to call you on your teasing, she has to do it in a respectful way. "Da-ad—you promised, right?" "Um, could you please not do that, Daddy? You said you wouldn't." Then treat her with the same consideration.

Where Do I Come In?

Nixing the teasing isn't an easy step because that kind of kidding comes naturally to a lot of guys. You have to pretty much deny a small part of your personality for the time being. But the other things you can do to help your tween daughter navigate her moods are actually easier because they're right down your alley. While her mother can probably relate more to the ups and downs, you're the one who can help her identify where they're coming from just by nature of being male and being The Dad.

First of all, you're way up there on her list of people she loves. She still wants your individual attention. Craves it. She *wants* you to hear and understand and respect her feelings even if she can't tell you that. And most of the time she can't. So—it's big when you're critical, or when you withhold affection, or when you try to explain her feelings away, or get testy with the way she's expressing them. All that to say, you've got the power to either guide her through the tough waters or drown her in them.

The power to guide comes from this fact: you, the dad, need ten words or less to understand what she's feeling. Her best friend, on the other hand, needs three paragraphs, which include not only what the issue is but the reassurance that she's loved and that things are going to be worked out between them.[10] You are, therefore, the perfect person to help her sort out what's going on with her emotions without a lot of extraneous stuff getting in the way.

At this point, you may be saying, "How am I supposed to do that when she doesn't stop talking long enough for me to get a word in?" Yeah, well, there's that. Girls' brains are organized for verbal mastery.[11] Talking is what they do, and, unlike us, they talk first and act later. So just remember this: girls are less likely than boys to end speaking by actually shutting up. When they've said all they have to say, they usually start repeating themselves.[12] When your daughter gets to the point where she's still saying words but not conveying a lot of new information, you can break in with something along these lines:

Do you want me to just listen, or are you interested in some suggestions?

Out of the Mouths of **Mini-Women**

I've really been trying to control my emotions, instead of yelling at my brothers and acting harsh to people. But if I do blow up or break down, my dad helps me get back in the middle. He comforts me and lets me explain what emotions I'm going through at that moment. If I don't feel like talking, he just sits with me. If I don't know how to explain what I'm feeling, he gives me a list of emotions, and I stop him when he gets to the one I'm feeling. Then I explain the whole thing to him. If I didn't have him, I don't know what would happen.

Can we just take a time-out here so I can ask a few questions?

Honey, I can't help you if I don't have a chance to say anything.

Okay, you're starting to lose me. Can we go back to that first thing you said and work on that?

Once you've got the floor, you can start helping her determine just exactly what she's feeling and why. A few tips on that:

Don't give her a lecture. Your maleness will want to kick in. In conversation, men do interrupt and hold forth much more than women,[13] but don't go there.

Instead, *ask questions*. Am I hearing a lot of anger in there? You pretty frustrated with your brother right now? Are you scared?

Once you determine together what's making her snarl at everybody in the house or sending her under the covers to sob, *don't tell her how she "should" feel*. Most of the time when we say, "That's the wrong way to feel," it's because the way she's feeling is making things harder for *us*. If she would just feel this way over here, you could get rid of the drama and get back to the playoffs. There are no "shoulds" in feelings. It is what it is, so work from there.

Don't make any feelings off-limits. It's okay for her to be heartbroken when her best friend moves away. Why wouldn't she get scared when she's going away from home for the first time or getting ready to have a tonsillectomy? What's off-limits is the idea that "If you were a good Christian, you wouldn't feel that way." Accepting Christ doesn't mean you stop being a feeling human being. Jesus didn't die to make us all robots. It's the way she expresses those feelings that's okay or not okay, that makes us good or not-so-good Christians. More on that in a minute.

Be extra careful not to squelch anger. When our sons blow a gasket over something, we get it. Getting mad is what men do. Matter of fact, about half the emotions we feel we express as anger. Grief, fear, frustration—it all comes out as "I'm royally ticked off." But when our daughters get angry, we think we have to defuse it. Anger from a girl seems "unfeminine" to us. We don't want our daughters to be little witches. But girls get angry, and well they should. Allow your daughter to be mad when she's mad. If anger seems "bad" to her, she's likely to think that *she*, therefore, is "bad." She'll stuff it and then blow over something totally unrelated and think she's a crazy person. The thing is, her anger is justified, just like yours is. It tells her something's wrong with the picture she's seeing. But like many women, she may have trouble expressing her anger to the person she's angry with for fear of losing their love. Most guys don't have that problem, so you're the one who can teach her appropriate ways to do that. As a result, she will very definitely not be a "witch."

When you do sit down to talk, *communicate face-to-face, literally.* Guys tend to prefer talking side by side. Face-to-face may seem adversarial to you, but to a girl, that's the sign of undivided attention.

With those guidelines in mind, you can meet the three mood challenges the dads of tween girls often find themselves faced with. In the process, you can have a huge influence on your daughter's emotional growth.

Challenge #1: Keeping the lines open

Despite the fact that you're the obvious candidate for helping your daughter muck through confusing feelings, and in spite of what we've said about her *wanting* your attention and your concern for her emotional state, she will sometimes act like you are *persona non grata* and head for her room. That's when it's tough, because you don't know whether she really wants to work things out for herself, which is a sign of growing maturity, or she wants you to follow her, knock on the door, and insist on a conversation.

There aren't any hard and fast rules on this. Just try to be available but not invasive. If you tell her on a regular basis that you're there for her if she needs to talk, and then you actually *are* there when she comes to you, she'll be more likely to do so. Especially if you don't push like an earthmover to get her to talk when she clams up.

Out of the Mouths of Mini-Women

I wish my dad understood me more. If I am upset and go to my room, he makes me come down and says how I should not act like a baby. Even if I don't feel like eating, he makes me.

I wish my dad understood that sometimes I need to go to my room and wallow in self-pity for a little bit and don't need to be mentored. I mean, I don't throw a pity party all day, but I need to just work everything out in my room.

Don't Say It, Dude ...

"We're going to sit here until you tell me what's wrong."
"Enough with the drama. What's going on?"
"All right, dish, baby girl. We don't keep secrets around here."
"Okay, it's time to stop crying and start talking."

Challenge #2: Keeping it civil

We touched on this previously, but it's worth elaborating on because we're hearing a lot of dads remark on how nasty their daughters' moods can get. We're talking abusive back talk, screaming, name-calling, hurling of projectiles. And it always blows both of us away when a parent says, "I don't know how she got that way."

She didn't get that way through some chance of genetics. Unless she's suffering from mental illness or reacting to childhood trauma, both of which you'd know about, she's mouthy and volatile because she's allowed to get away with it. Opinionated. Extroverted. Passionate. Those are inborn traits. Disrespectful, careless with people's feelings, rude, arrogant—those are permitted behaviors that need to be *un*-permitted, and can be.

And, listen, that's not an attack on your parenting so far. Your daughter may have been a pure delight until she hit puberty, and now you're paddling like mad just to catch up. Or maybe her precocious mouthy-ness was cute when she was little and is now so obnoxious you can't stand it. Or maybe you just assumed this kind of behavior was normal for a tween and that she'll just grow out of it. It isn't, and chances are she won't.

So what to do? Suddenly declare a dictatorship? Kick tail and take names?

True, you do have to take back control, but not in a controlling way, if that makes sense. If it doesn't, this may help:

Do not *tell yourself it's too late.* At nine, ten, eleven, or twelve, she's not so far gone in her insolence that you can't pull her back. She actually wants you to. Seriously—nobody's happy when they're always in a foul mood, constantly ready to attack everybody. She may act like you're ruining her life when you start insisting on respect, but it's exactly that. An act. Besides, as comedienne Carol Burnett once said when she was in the throes of issues with her daughter, "Sometimes you have to love your kids enough to let them hate you for a while."

Make it clear with a direct statement that you will not be verbally abused. That should come before any consequences. While a lot of tweens will test that, some will take you at your word and shape up immediately, like they were just waiting for you to say something. Be specific about what you won't tolerate. (See the list on page 58.) Be firm, civil, and non-threatening. It's just a statement of fact, not open to discussion. Period.

Establish what the consequences are going to be for those behaviors and stick to them. Taking away Internet privileges, grounding from activities she loves, canceling BFF visits—those are effective. Physical punishment is not. As for yelling: it isn't even a consequence; it's just something she'll get through until you stop. About halfway into your tirade, she's no longer listening anyway. She's watching your veins bulge or wondering why you get to yell and scream but she doesn't.

Speaking of which, if you want her to stop being verbally abusive to *you*, don't be verbally abusive to *her*. Yeah, you're the parent and she's the kid, but in this case you're modeling behavior that she can't help but copy. If you swear and rant at her, you can't reasonably expect her to express her anger at you in any other way. *Fathers, don't exasperate your children* . . .

If she does break the rules and blow up in your face, *don't over-react, even though you want to take her flip-flop and smack her with it.* This is a good place to talk about physical punishment. It's the worst way you can deal with your daughter—and here's where another passage of Scripture gets grossly misused. "He who spares the rod hates his son" (Proverbs 13:24) does not mean grab a rod and whale the tar out of your kid with it. The "rod" in question is the shepherd's rod, with which he guides his flock, gently. Hence the Twenty-third Psalm and the image of Jesus as the Good Shepherd. The shepherd never beats his sheep.

Not only that, but what kind of message are you sending your daughter when you spank or slap her? That it's okay for someone who loves her, especially a man, to hit her? And forget "This hurts me more than it hurts you." If it hurt you, you wouldn't do it. You're venting your own anger, and the result is either resentment on the part of your daughter, the very thing you're trying to avoid, or her conviction that a man stronger than her has the right to smack her when he loses patience.

Out of the Mouths of Mini-Women

Sometimes my dad can be really nice. But he yells a lot. I can't stand yelling. His temper is like a pot of boiling water and you never know when it's going to boil over. I think my dad is a huge wimp and he tries to cover it by yelling. The only thing is, he doesn't know how he makes me feel or how many times he makes me cry.

Haul in a deep breath instead and, as calmly as possible, tell her she's blown it and there are going to be consequences. Bring them on immediately without discussion or negotiation. If she throws a full-blown tantrum, ask her to go pull herself together, and then when she calms down, you can discuss whatever it was that brought on her meltdown. The consequences, however, still stand.

Expect an apology. Asking for one isn't going to do it, and accepting "Okay, I'm SOR-ry" with accompanying eye roll won't change future behavior. The way to get a genuine apology is to (a) apologize to her when *you* make a mistake and (b) accept any heartfelt apology with a hug and no further discussion of the subject unless she still has questions. Let it go. Move on.

Challenge #3. Keeping a difference of opinion from turning into an argument

There's no denying it was easier back when she took every word you said as gospel. If you were lucky enough to have a daughter like that. I, uh, didn't. Marijean argued with me before she could actually say words. Pointing her little index finger and wrinkling her brow, she'd let me have it with a tirade of gibberish that made me glad I didn't know what she was saying. I knew I was in trouble.

So I know whereof I speak when I tell you that your tween daughter *is* going to start having opinions of her own if she doesn't already and that you *can* discuss those with her without winding up purple in the face. I had to learn that the hard way. Marijean would come home with some ridiculous piece of misinformation she picked up from some friend who supposedly knew all, and I'd immediately come at her with, "What are you *talking* about?" Or "Where'd you hear *that*?" She'd go on the defensive and I'd drive harder to make the point that she didn't know a thing about whatever it was. It usually happened at the dinner table ... which could account for about half those times she ran crying to her room. I thought I was saving her from making an idiot out of herself, and she thought I was telling her she *was* an idiot. Thinking about it now, I wish I'd paid more attention to the bullets Nancy was shooting at me with her eyes. What would I have done differently? What, actually, *did* I learn to do ... eventually?

Validate her thoughts even if you don't agree with them. "I can see how you'd think that, but ..." "I never heard that before." Or even an interested, "Really." She needs to know it's okay for her to have an opinion, and it is. Get over being the unquestioned authority on everything, or it'll come back to bite you.

Ask her questions about what she's bringing to the table. Love this quote from Generation Y expert Amy Lynch: "Questions act like speed bumps on the highway to verbal collisions."[14] Saying, "Can you talk to me some more about _____?" lets your daughter know you're actually interested in her point of view and that you want to connect with her. Asking a question also slows you down and keeps you from overreacting. You have to be careful, of course, about how you ask. "Where in the world did you come up with *that*?" isn't really a question. It's more like an attack on her intelligence. Okay, yeah, she's only just learning how to form opinions from data, but making her feel like an airhead isn't going to teach her how to do that.

Help her explain her opinions. Nancy taught me this. She'd say, "Tell me some more, Marijean," and as the thing unfolded, I'd see where Mj was coming from, which didn't happen when I was over there telling her how ridiculous she was being. Again, questions are good, and so is restating, as in, "So what I think you're saying is _____." One dad says to his daughter, "Okay, tell me what you know. Then I'll tell you what I know. Fair enough?" Next time, she'll be clearer because you've shown her how to *be* clearer.

Show respect for the differences between you. Seriously, do you have to win every discussion? Does there even have to be a winner and a loser? It's more about the sharing of ideas than a declaration of who's right and who's wrong. If her opinion is dangerous—she's heard recreational drugs are okay, for instance—go ahead and set her straight (without implying that she's a moron for even considering it). But if she thinks the Jonas Brothers are to die for and you think they're little twerps, do you have to run it into the ground until she's in tears? She's figuring out who she is—and she's not you.

For Pete's sake, don't withdraw affection because she disagrees with you. Giving her the silent treatment or going all brusque on her makes her wonder what she did wrong. Worse, she'll think having an opinion, to disagree—to grow up—is a bad thing. Do you really want her to stop expressing her thoughts and feelings to you, just to be sure she doesn't make you not love her anymore? It sounds ridiculous to you, but that's what's going on in her head. Even if you blow the whole conversation, make sure you tell her you love her before you end it. Do it even if she doesn't respond. Be the grown-up.

Bridging the Gap

Father, my daughter's moods are zig-zagging all over the place, and she always seems to be zigging when I'm zagging. Please bridge the gap between what she needs in those times and what I have to offer to help her through them. Can't do it alone. Counting on you, Father.
Amen.

4

We Need Another Bathroom

What Just Happened?

You're up on the ladder, painting the living room ceiling, when your wife and daughter come home from shopping. You hear the giggling, and it occurs to you that it's getting harder to tell whose giggle is whose. You also hear the rattling of bags and try not to wonder how much that shopping spree just cost you.

A door closes down the hall, only slightly muffling the laughing and whispering and crinkling of tissue paper. Tissue paper. Not good. Only the pricier stores wrap stuff in tissue paper. You tell yourself to be appropriately impressed when your wife does her usual post-mall fashion show and wait till she's through before you ask to see the credit card receipts. At least you've learned a couple of things in umpty-ump years of marriage.

You dip your brush in the paint and refocus, but the door opens again and eager footsteps tap down the hall. It only just begins to register that they belong not to your wife but to your daughter, when your daughter asks, "What do you think, Dad?"

You glance under your arm in time to see her twirl across the paint-spattered drop cloth, price tags flapping. Oh, so *she* got the new clothes. Kids' stuff is cheaper, right?

You smile as you drag the brush with expert precision along the edge of the ceiling. "You look like my little princess," you say automatically.

"Dad."

I do think my dad thinks I'm beautiful, but he doesn't really show it. Sometimes I wish he would just come right out and say it.

You stifle a sigh and look down. She stands below you, hands on her hips.

"I'm not a little princess anymore," she says.

You are to me, you start to say. And then you take another—okay, your *first* real look at what she's displaying. Some kind of tight black pants with a mini-jeans-skirt over them and a purple top thing that fits her like a second skin and a scarf thrown around her neck.

She's right. She doesn't look like a little princess.

"How come it's not pink?" you say.

"Dad? Seriously?"

"You always wear pink."

"Not any *more*." She flops her hands out to her sides and looks at you expectantly.

You know you better say something and it better be right. You're about to comment that you're glad she's wearing pants under that skirt when your gaze lands on her feet.

"Are those *heels*?" you say.

"Kitten heels," she says. "They're just little."

The recent memory of her randomly falling spread-eagle across the kitchen floor flashes through your mind. "Can you even walk in those?" you say.

"Yes, Dad." You see her consciously suppress an eye roll as she turns and strolls back across the drop cloth, making her way gracefully amid the paint cans. When did this child get mini-hips? And when did she learn to sway them like that?

She turns, waiting, and you have a sudden glimpse into the future that you weren't expecting today. How much it all costs is now obliterated by what it all means. Until you can figure it out, you decide to fall back on what almost always works.

"Stop it," you say. "Stop growing up right now."

You grin at her. She doesn't grin back. The disappointment in her eyes makes you want to stick your head in your paint bucket.

————

I guess we know in theory that our little girls are going to grow into women, but for the most part we're pretty much in denial about it. But when your daughter starts taking an interest in her appearance, and that appearance starts changing, like, overnight, it's pretty hard to keep believing she's always going to be your little princess or your tomboy in a ponytail or, as in my case, your consummate dreamer caught up in a world she made up herself.

It's pretty hard to miss when the behavior of her hair becomes an issue and a trip to Target for some new T-shirts turns into the Louisiana Purchase. There's no denying she's turning into a mini-woman when her brother is hollering outside the bathroom door while she's in there doing whatever it is females do for an hour every time they get out of the shower. You can tell your son that it's a mystery to mankind and not to try to figure it out, but *you* pretty much need to figure out (a) the part that makes this such a pivotal time for your daughter as she develops her view of herself, and (b) the part you play in that.

My dad tells me I'm beautiful, and I believe him.

Here's the Deal

Before we start, we need to get clear on the fact that what your daughter thinks of the way she looks *does* matter. The biggest mistake you can make in this area is to tell her that the *only* thing that's important is who she is on the inside, and that she shouldn't put *any* emphasis on her physical appearance. Come on, are you serious?

We're going to spend time on inner beauty in this chapter. We can't help it, actually, because who anybody is "within" has a huge impact on how attractive they are "without." And whether a girl feels beautiful on the outside affects her behavior from the inside. But for now, just put aside any urge you may have to say, "I'm not getting into this beauty thing at all. I just want her to develop good character," and look at where she's coming from so you're prepared to help her with both.

Three things come into play to shape your daughter's image of what she looks like.

#1. What comes naturally

Nobody tells an eight-year-old girl to gaze in the mirror and wonder if she's pretty (that, by the way, accounts for some of the post-shower hours she spends in the bathroom). A nine-year-old female doesn't have a guidebook that instructs her to experiment with her mother's makeup so she'll see what she's going to look like someday. And there is definitely nobody instructing the eleven-year-old to freak out because she discovers pimples dotting her chin. All of that is a natural function of being female, and although it happens in varying degrees according to individual personality, it comes with her gender. She isn't self-obsessed. She isn't trying to skip her childhood. She isn't destined to become a shallow fashionista. She's just being a girl. Here's what's normal for her tween age.

An inconsistent interest in her appearance. One day she spends an entire afternoon cleaning out her closet and trying on outfits. The next she's back in her sweats and tennies, shooting baskets with her brothers. She begs to be allowed to wear the ballet flats to church because they totally go with her outfit, but you spot her after the service, shoeless, climbing on the monkey bars. She has to have the sparkly bracelets her BFFs are wearing and dons them with a T-shirt and shorts. Those are all good signs that she's figuring out how to be attractive and still be herself. Don't try to keep up.

And don't be concerned if your daughter doesn't turn into a girly-girl. She may not obsess over having the right 'do and may be able to pass a Claire's without a second glance. But if you pay attention, you'll see that she likes to have just the right tennis shoes or that the number of favorite T-shirts has doubled. Even tomboys like to look good.

An increase in the amount of time it takes her to get ready to go somewhere. Where your wife used to have to hogtie the child just to brush her hair, now she's the one still primping her ponytail when you already have the motor running. There's an outfit to pick out—and maybe change once or twice—a purse to pack—hair to wrestle into place. It isn't as easy for her as it used to be, and it's all new, so it takes a while to make it happen. When she gets into the upper range of her tweens and starts shaving her legs, maybe using some lip gloss, and possibly medicating what to you are microscopic zits, you might want to rip your hair out, if you have any left by then. As one dad told us, "It's so much easier to leave the house with boys."

At least the occasional disagreement with her mother over her appearance. It's part of her normal differentiation between herself and everybody else to say, "I hate pink now," just because her mother has suggested she wear it. She isn't being consciously contrary; she's just trying to find out exactly who she is, and her taste is part of that.

Differences in opinion over what's appropriate are bound to arise too. Nancy has always been one to like to dress up whenever the occasion calls for it. Marijean, not so much. I remember one night when Mj was eleven—Nancy was taking her to the ballet, which Marijean was excited about until Nancy told her she had to wear a dress. A battle ensued that turned into a standoff. Marijean wasn't going if she had to get dressed up, and Nancy wasn't taking her if she didn't. I remember hoping I wasn't going to be expected to go in her place.

Throw in disputes over what the ubiquitous "everybody else" is wearing and you've got the makings of World Wrestling Entertainment. As we've said before, just because arguing over clothes and makeup (*make*up?!) and haircuts is normal pushing-of-the-envelope doesn't mean you should shrug and hope she'll grow out of it. We'll talk about how to referee or, even better, avoid daily reruns of Smackdown. Just know that your daughter's not headed for juvie just because she fights your wife on the length of her skirt.

Some self-deprecation. Yeah, don't worry if your daughter's image of herself isn't always positive. Have you ever known a woman who was completely happy with the way she looked 24/7? Expect some self-critiquing of things you can't see even after she points them out to you—frizzy hair (didn't we used to call them curls?), the worst fingernails on the entire planet (she's seen every fingernail on the planet?), the even grosser acne (one pimple makes it acne?). Most of the time when she bewails the things that render her, in her opinion, butt-ugly, she's just venting and will be perfectly happy with her sweet self five minutes later. She may also be looking for reassurance that she's not the most hideous child you've ever seen and should be wearing a bag over her head.

#2. What the world is telling her

We've already talked about the way the marketers have honed in on the "tween buying machine." Couple that with the belief embraced by product developers that each new generation wants to push the limits further than the one before it, and you've got a society that's saying to your nine-year-old daughter, "You need to look like a teenager or you are not okay."

Right this minute, we're looking at a quiz in a magazine designed for tween girls, entitled "Who's Your Celeb Fashion Inspiration?" The four choices are Miranda Cosgrove, Demi Lovato, Taylor Swift, and Selena Gomez. If you even know who any of those people are, you're doing better than I am. The point is, the eight- to twelve-year-old girl reading that can determine whether she is casual chic, has a funky and original sense of style, goes totally glam, or is consistently trendy. There's nothing actually wrong with that. Nancy talks about personal style in *The Beauty Book* and *The Skin You're In*, both of which are best-sellers with tween girls. The point is, there's a whole lot more emphasis on what to wear than there used to be at this age. If your daughter isn't into that yet, she can come home from school feeling very uncool. If, on the other hand, she's determined to *be* cool, she might buy into the trend toward looking way more grown up than she is.

Some companies are paying attention to that. JCPenney, for instance, has a line of tween girls' (and boys') clothing known as Uproar, for what they call "aspirational" tweens—kids who adopt fashion early but can't wear the low-cut tops or edgy graphics designed for teens. Other retailers are going with the KGOY (Kids Getting Older Younger) thing and providing sophisticated teen styles in girls' sizes. So with the mall, the magazines, and the music videos all telling your still-a-little-girl daughter that she needs to look like jail bait, she has to learn early that what "they" say is beautiful isn't necessarily who she wants to be. That's a lot to handle when you're ten years old.

Her friends and peers are part of that world as well. It really wouldn't matter if her BFFs or the "popular" girls were wearing garbage bags cinched at the waist with their dads' belts—she'd feel at least some pressure to wear that too. She might eschew the trend and wear what she wants, and more power to her if she does, but she's going to be teased or at the very least whispered about, and it's the rare tween who can endure that without some self-doubt. Even if she wears the very same style tee or tank or leggings as Miss Thing in her class, but Miss Thing's comes from Limited II and your daughter's was purchased at Walmart, there's going to be flack.

It isn't only in the fashion realm that she's getting the idea that she has to be "perfect." Both critical (and sometimes cruel) kids and the media offer up the notion that the following are required in order to be considered beautiful:

A body like a model (which is 25 to 30 percent thinner than the average girl[1]).

Flawless skin (which even the heavily Photoshopped models don't actually have).

Thick, shiny, and preferably blonde hair (ditto that Photoshopping comment).

Legs up to your neck.

Manicured nails (at fifty bucks a pop).

Teeth so white they're almost blue.

We'll stop there before you get nauseous. It's ridiculous, completely unattainable, but that's what's being held up as the "standard" for our daughters. Do you know *anyone* who measures up to that? For that matter, do you *want* to know a woman who spends the kind of time on herself that it takes to get there, much less stay there? Yet that's what our daughters are told they have to go by, which means the chances of them feeling fat and ugly most of the time are pretty high. Makes you want to punch somebody out.

#3. What she gets from you, Dad

You may have taken a vow of silence on this whole thing — decided to leave it entirely up to your daughter's mom so you won't get yourself into trouble. If you've done that, you're already *in* trouble, because your daughter's basic reassurance that she is transforming into a beautiful young woman comes from you. Your "no comment" means to her that she's not worth commenting on.

You might think this is such a woman thing that the onus naturally falls on the mom. But what your daughter's mother says about *herself* has more of an influence on your daughter's self-image than

My dad tells me I'm beautiful a lot! When I'm all dressed up for church or something like that, he'll even start singing, "Hey, good lookin'" — the way dads do.

what she says about your child. (If your svelte wife says, "I'm so fat," fifteen times a day, your pubescently chubby daughter will be convinced she must be the Goodyear blimp.) What *you* say about your *daughter* has that same kind of bearing. You are the first and at this point the most important man in her life. She's already figured out, even if unconsciously, that it's the men she needs to please, not the other women, so it only makes sense that if you tell her she's drop-dead gorgeous, she'll be inclined to believe it. If you constantly point out that she's chunky or boyish or the Smart One (as opposed to her sister, the Pretty One), she'll believe that too. And don't think for a minute that she won't.

My dad will say, "Holly, stop being cute," and I'll put on my "totally cute" look, and he'll chuckle.

In Reality

Consider this an attitude check. Mark each of the following statements that is true for you. We've put them into two categories, one referring to your tween daughter and one to your view of women in general. We'll let you draw your own conclusions from your answers.

Your view of your daughter:

- ○ I think she's an adorable little girl.
- ○ I think she's growing into a beautiful young woman.
- ○ I think she's going through an ugly duckling phase, but she's going to be good-looking at the other end of it.
- ○ I think she's an average-looking kid, and I don't see that as a problem.
- ○ I think she's too cute for her own good.
- ○ I'm a little concerned that she's on the homely side, and I wonder if she's ever going to grow into herself.
- ○ I don't really pay that much attention to her appearance.

Your view of women in general:

- ○ I think they're all beautiful in their own way.
- ○ I think only the near-perfect women can actually be called beauties.

○ I think most women who are considered beautiful tend to be shallow and self-centered.

○ I think any woman can be beautiful if she fixes herself up.

○ I think any woman is more beautiful when she goes natural.

○ I would never be attracted to a woman who wasn't pretty.

○ I would never be attracted to a woman who didn't keep herself well-groomed.

○ I think it's unbiblical for women to be concerned about their appearance.

○ I appreciate it when women take the time to look good.

○ It's hard for me to take cute girls and women seriously.

You might want to refer to the statements you marked as you read on. They'll definitely influence the way you show your daughter that she's beautiful.

Learning from the Master

Those of you guys who are totally into your Bibles have probably had 1 Peter 3:3–4 flashing in your head the whole time we've been talking. For those less apt to quote chapter and verse, it goes like this:

> *Wives ... your beauty should not come from outward adornment, such as braided hair and the wearing of gold jewelry and fine clothes. Instead, it should be that of your inner self, the unfading beauty of a gentle and quiet spirit, which is of great worth in God's sight.*
>
> 1 Peter 3:1,3–4

It's another one of those passages that frequently gets taken out of context and used to shame people—in this case, tween girls who are just becoming aware of their blossoming beauty and are told to forget the pierced ears and the cute haircut and concentrate on their "gentle and quiet spirit."

In the first place, if you have an eight- to twelve-year-old daughter with a gentle and quiet spirit, you are one in ten thousand. You practically won the lottery, dude. Not that the rest of us would trade our continually chattering, constantly moving, emotionally bouncing girl-children for anyone else, but a little gentleness and quiet would

Mini-Women

Mostly my dad is prompted by my mom to say I'm beautiful. She'll say, "Isn't our daughter so pretty?" and he'll respond, "Yep." But he encourages me to live life in a beautiful and Christlike way. He helps me to appreciate inner beauty more than outer, and when he says he's proud of me, that's when I know he thinks I'm truly beautiful.

be nice once in a while. Tell her she needs to be soft-spoken and tender, and she's liable to look at you like you're insane. Seriously, Dad?

In the second place, Peter isn't saying your daughter should never braid her hair or put on a 23 karat necklace or wear that cute get-up Grandma sent. He's saying that isn't what makes her beautiful in God's eyes or, truth be told, in anybody else's either. The real stuff—the shining eyes, the be-still-my-heart smile, the glowing cheeks, the happy way she tosses her hair when she likes somebody—that's all a reflection of what's going on inside, and it is stunning.

In the third place, Peter isn't suggesting that all girls' personalities be exactly alike—everybody demure and whispery with eyes downcast. There is more than one way to be gentle and quiet inside. Your daughter might be the proverbial life of the party, and if there isn't a party, she'll create one. Which is not to say that she isn't at peace with herself, or that she wouldn't abandon the whole shindig to be gentle to the wallflower in the corner.

"In God's sight" are the operative words in the passage. Not "in her BFF's sight." Not "in some absurd little creep boy's sight." Not even "in the church's sight." Her at-peace, loving spirit is what is of worth to God—and whatever that looks like in and on your daughter is her own particular brand of beauty. For any community to say, "She should not wear makeup or have cute hair, and should be seen and not heard," isn't biblical, any more than "If she looks good, who cares what's going on in her heart?" is. What's beautiful *on* your daughter is what is real *in* her. That's inner beauty. Anything she does in terms of appearance, from her barrettes to her flip-flops, should reflect it.

Whatever you can do to help her embrace that, do it. We've got some suggestions for you.

Where Do I Come In?

There are probably, to use tween language, "a million things!" you could do to insure that your influence is positive. We've narrowed them down to six.

Take an interest without being invasive. Different parts of that are hard for different guys. If you barely notice what your wife is wearing, much less your nine-year-old, it won't be too tough for you to avoid being invasive, but you might have trouble remembering to give a compliment. If you routinely critique your wife's outfits and hair color, taking an interest in your daughter's appearance will be like breathing for you, but you might have to watch yourself so you don't wind up stumbling into her territory.

How to show your tween daughter that you care about her appearance? That can be anything from making it a point to notice when she's wearing something new (even if she says, "Dad, I wear this every *day*!") to helping her pick out something when she's lamenting that she doesn't have anything to wear. (Women seem to emerge from the womb with that complaint.) You can tell her what colors you like on her, or comment on how grown-up that haircut makes her look, or remark that she has great skin like Aunt Somebody (making sure first that she hasn't taken Aunt Somebody off her Most Admired list).

If you don't think to do that on your own, at least give her your undivided attention when she asks you for input. Actually look up from the laptop if she wants to know if you like her new jacket. Look at her for more than five seconds if she wants your opinion on her every-nail-a-different-color manicure. She's not asking for a full fashion review. She just wants you to see her. If we don't have time to do that for our daughters, we're over-committed.

I admit I wasn't always the most attentive father when Marijean was a tween, but some of the best times we had together were when we went shopping. I dug that for some reason. I think it was an easy way to show her that I knew who she was. From the time she could talk, she made it clear she didn't like frills and ruffles. At age three, she'd walk through the kids' department feeling articles of clothing, and when she found one that wasn't "scratchy" she'd say, "I like this." Ruffles were scratchy. And not her.

She was never a doll we could dress up. She had a definite personality from day one. So I'd find things that were her flavor—things she could move around in, things that didn't restrict her super-active imagination, things that said, "I am not fluffy—take me seriously." We'd pick out cool jackets and a lot of denim with embroidered stuff

Mini-Women

My dad TOTALLY thinks I'm beautiful! He's told me a million times! And not in a lying tone! In a way serious tone! I love my dad!

on it and long sweaters (it was the '80s, okay?). Forget shoulder pads and big polka dots and hair bows (again, it was the '80s). We never stood in the aisle and argued. I never shook my head when she came out of the dressing room and twirled (tween girls twirl no matter who they are). For two people who had a debate over just about everything else, those were good times.

You might be more inclined to poke a fork in your eye than go shopping with your daughter, but I'm just saying, look for a way to bring your natural instincts to the table with hers. She isn't expecting anything in particular. She just wants to know that you notice her and that you like what you see.

What she *doesn't* want is for you to tell her what she will and will not wear, period, end of discussion. If you have concerns about skirt length and neckline dip, that kind of thing, sit down with her and her mom and make some firm guidelines that she can then work within. Maybe it'll be no skirts more than a hand's width above her knees—no sweat pants with stuff printed across the seat—nothing so tight you can read the labels on her underwear. Make sure she gets why you're setting those parameters, and then let her choose from the options that fall within them. There won't be any fitting room arguments or sulking in the car because she didn't get the T-shirt that says "I'm a Brat" in glitter on the front. If she has some input in coming up with those guidelines, you won't be the bad guy. You'll just be the dad who cares.

Help her strike a balance between taking pride in her appearance and freaking out over every little flaw in it. Once she starts noticing her own skin and hair and freckle situation, there are bound to be times when those things are gigantic to her. She doesn't want to go to her BFF's pool party because her swimsuit is "stupid" (i.e., it isn't a bikini, which is what *all* the other girls have—*all* of them). She tries on six different outfits while you're waiting, sunglasses on, keys in hand, blood pressure rising. She bursts into tears in the car on the way to school because she has to give a speech in front of the class and her teeth are yellow, which she knows because the girl whose father is a dentist told her so. This beauty thing is all new to her so it may take her a while to gain perspective. She needs you to draw the

Mini-Women

My dad commonly comments on how nice I look or how he likes my hair or my jeans or whatever. My mom and I often ask him which outfit looks better. My dad really likes me to feel good about myself, I know that.

line at what's excessive, which you'll get best results with if you keep your sense of humor in the midst of the drama.

> If anybody stands up in the middle of your speech and points at your teeth, you have my word that we will move so you can change schools.
>
> I have the perfect solution: I'll come in and pick an outfit for you.
>
> You want to try on something of mine?
>
> It was torture for me too when my mom wouldn't let me wear a bikini.

Do it with a grin and a hug and no sarcasm. Make sure she knows you're not laughing at her. Don't minimize her pain in other things that really do matter, but in this case, when you're trying to help her get perspective, ya gotta nudge her away from taking herself too seriously.

There are two great ways to avoid those scenes all together. One is to talk about the fakey-phony-plastic way women on TV and movies often look, especially when you're watching together. Point out the beauty hype in commercials and encourage her to point it out to you. Be her ally in seeing it for what it is and refusing to buy into it. That also means being careful about the comments you make about women you know or see, whether your daughter is with you or not.

The other is to talk to her a lot about what she thinks and believes, what she feels and dreams and loves to do, rather than dwell entirely on how she looks. "You are adorable in that outfit," takes seven seconds. "Is there much bullying at your school?" could win you a half-hour conversation, in which she'll feel special because you care what she thinks. Special comes out as beautiful.

Never let her rely on her pretty charm to manipulate you. We can't state that any better than Don Elium does in his book *Raising a Daughter.* He says, "We as fathers … fail to hold girls accountable for their mistakes, because they're so cute."[2] If you're firmly wrapped around your daughter's little finger, now's the time to get untangled and hold her to the rules and guidelines of your house. If you don't, you're sending the message that her beauty and her ability to use it to her advantage will get her whatever she wants. It won't always,

Mini-Women

My dad doesn't want me not to care at all about how I look and just wear whatever I want, but he also doesn't want me to care TOO much about how I look.

for openers, and why would she develop any real character knowing she had that going for her? Think of it this way: are you going to let her charm you into buying her booze or letting her stay out all night when she's a teenager? No brainer. But try waiting until then to stop letting her work you and watch World War III commence.

Be authentic in your praise. Your tween daughter knows genuine when she hears it and she prides herself on being able to say, "That is so fake." That's exactly what you're teaching her to do. So it doesn't make sense to hand out compliments you don't really mean, which is actually worse than not saying anything at all. These are the kinds of things she'll see through like Saran Wrap:

Don't Say It, Dude ...

"You're the most beautiful girl in the world."
"You're prettier than all the other girls in your class."
"Nobody's even going to notice your pimples."
"You're perfect."

If you want to say, "*As far as I'm concerned*, you're the most beautiful girl in the world," you can get away with that, but she knows she's not *the* most beautiful, and besides, the comparison thing sets up a whole other set of problems. A simple "Are you gorgeous tonight or what?" is more personal and believable anyway. You do want her to believe everything you say to her, and this is no exception.

Help her overcome beauty barriers. Things like glasses (which only *she* sees as an obstacle to beauty) or facial scars (which *everybody* sees as one). Maybe she has a lazy eye or a birthmark or teeth that are going to require years of orthodontia. Telling her it doesn't matter is a lie. Telling her she can still be beautiful in spite of it is the truth. You can follow up by helping her

not to be self-conscious, which is never a good look for anybody.

to have a sense of humor about it, with funny comebacks at the ready for anybody rude enough to try to embarrass her by

---

Mini-Women

Every time I want to dye my hair or change the way I look, my dad hugs me and tells me how beautiful I am to God. And then I thank God for giving me a dad who loves me and thinks I'm beautiful in every way.

pointing it out. "Yeah, I can pick up hundreds of radio stations with these braces." "Pizza Face? How clever."

not to bring undue attention to it. "You're staring at my weird eye, aren't you?"

to play up all her other great qualities, in her appearance and her personality.

to realize that once people get to know and like her, they don't even notice it anymore.

to look forward to the time when it will be fixed (the braces are off, she's old enough for contacts, the other kids will catch up to her in height), without hiding in the closet until that day comes.

She may also come up with imagined beauty bummers that nobody else really sees as a problem. The family nose her face hasn't caught up to yet. Bright red hair women pay big bucks to achieve chemically. A multitude of curls (more big bucks). Full lips (has she never *heard* of Angelina Jolie?). Reassure her once that it's no big deal to anyone else. When she brings it up again, tell her you're only hearing new business today. On the side, talk to her mother about any self-deprecating *she* does in front of your daughter. By constantly complaining about her hips and her thighs and the texture of her skin, Mom is modeling the brutal self-critiquing you're trying to prevent. Again, what her mother says about *herself* has more of an impact on your daughter than any compliments she gives her.

Bridging the Gap

Father, creator of my beautiful daughter, she's growing up in a beauty culture you *didn't* create, and I hate it for her. Please bridge the gap between the image of herself you want her to see and my ability to make her see it. Can't do it alone. Counting on you, Father.

Amen.

Mini-Women

I think my dad thinks I'm beautiful. He tells me that all the time. I admit that sometimes I don't believe him when he says it, and I'll think, Oh, he's just saying that because he's my dad, but I know he wouldn't lie to me.

5

Who Is She Today?

What Just Happened?

You've been elected to drive your daughter to a Saturday afternoon birthday party, which is really okay. You like listening to her jack her jaws in the car. Last time you took her someplace, you got the complete scoop on everything that was going down on your street — including people you didn't even know lived there. Since this party is across town where a former best friend has moved to, you could get the 411 on the entire neighborhood.

But today she's quiet. She slumps in the seat, clutching a gift bag that spews forth pink tissue paper and jittering her feet just above the floorboard. Your attempts at conversation — "How's school?" — "How was soccer practice?" — even "How 'bout those Mets?" are answered with, "Fine." "Okay, I guess." And "I don't know." All in a meek little voice, without an eye roll in sight. Something is clearly up.

By the time you pull up to the curb in front of former BFF's house, where pink balloons have been tied to the mailbox, your daughter's chin is quivering and she makes no move to open the car door.

"What's wrong, kiddo?" you ask.

The answer spills out along with the tears. "I don't want to go."

"How come?" you say. "What's going on?"

"I won't know anybody."

"You know —"

"I mean besides her. And I don't even know *her* anymore. What if she changed since she moved?"

My daddy doesn't really, really know who I am. I'm not even sure I know who I really, really am.

You have the good sense not to point out that "she" just moved a month ago. Instead, you cup your child's chin and you smile at her and say, "You're gonna be fine. Just go in there and be yourself."

This does not compel her to leap from the vehicle with a brand-new attitude. She looks at you, eyes brimming.

"I don't know how to do that," she says.

"Don't know how to do what?" you say.

"I don't know how to be myself."

She swallows and blinks and stares down into the abyss of pink tissue, and you have a stunning insight. She doesn't know how to be herself because your bright, sunny, used-to-be-confident daughter suddenly doesn't know who she is.

And you don't have a clue what to tell her.

———————

Mini-Women

My dad lets me be myself, I think. But that's tough because I'm still trying to figure out who I am!

We are now heading into some of the roughest territory in tween-dom: the realm of authenticity. Who is she now and how can she be true to that and still fit in? They're confusing questions for her, and it's vital that she discover a way to find the answers, because she's going to have to find them over and over again throughout her life as who she is and how she fits in change over time. And just like everything else we've talked about, society will try to tell her who she "should" be. So will her friends, her teachers, her coaches, and her siblings. It's up to the two people who know her best to help her make her way through all of that to her true self. One's her mom. The other's you.

But, man, this is tough for a dad. You used to have Child Daughter pretty well pegged. But the little princess is now a tween drama queen. The tiny tough tomboy is now a powerhouse. The sunny, funny junior comedienne is now a sarcastic social critic. Or is she? Just when you think you have *New* Daughter correctly pigeonholed, she discards that self and tries on a new one, sometimes with all the confidence of a Harvard MBA, at other times with bunny-like timidity.

You can wind up feeling completely out of touch with her, and where before you were the daddy who had all the answers, you now don't have an inkling what they are. Matter of fact, you might not even know what the questions are, because neither does she. Every girl is unique both in her self-ness and in her method of uncovering it, so we can't tell you exactly what to do to get back in the loop where you can help her. We do have some guidelines, though. We'll start by explaining what's going on with tween girls in general at this stage.

Here's the Deal

You have to go on a girl-by-girl basis with this, but for the most part, a tween girl knows *she doesn't want to be a little kid anymore.* Anything babyish is completely taboo. Again, what is considered "too young" varies with the individual, but there are certain things that just aren't going to be part of her particular life now. Watching what she discards can tell you a lot. She might turn her back on the whole doll thing or decide riding her bike is no longer cool or put all her picture books in a pile and announce that they need to go to the Goodwill. You can accept it the same way you did the passing away of diapers and bottles and that disgusting blanket she dragged around with her.

The goal ahead of her is to be sixteen. There's something magical to a girl about that distant age, as if the pumpkin's going to turn into a carriage and carry her off to the ball. Hence experimenting with makeup at sleepovers and developing crushes on boy bands.

The issue for the tween girl is that *she doesn't know how to get there or who to be in the meantime.* And since she's unique unto herself, she has to go through a lot of trial and error, put on and take off different versions of herself, and figure out what parts of her are false layers she's piled on to survive school and older brothers and all the other girls who are trying to do the same thing.

That could actually be a lot of fun for her—and sometimes is. But she's faced with a number of obstacles that keep her from either finding the real her or having the courage to *be* her. To name a few:

Being expected to grow up too fast. Not to run this one into the ground, but once again it comes up. If she accepts the you're-just-a-small-teenager thing, or her time is so structured and demanding she doesn't have time to explore herself, she'll miss the whole process. She may be at the top level in her dance studio at age eleven

Mini-Women

My dad knows who I really am. He's like an expert on me. It's like he has a sixth sense to know who's really me.

Mini-Women

I love my dad and he helps me with a lot of stuff — but let's face it, he's male. He's never going to completely understand all that I do and say.

without ever examining whether she really likes ballet. She may don the expected teen togs without even seeing clothes that actually fit her personality. She might feel so pressured to make top grades, she doesn't experience any carefree hours to grow into herself. Playing and daydreaming are part of a child's development, and a girl between the ages of eight and twelve is still a child. Put an iPhone in her hand and replace her Nancy Drew books with a CD collection, and she's going to lose sight of that. Not a good thing.

Borrowing identities from celebrities. It's always been normal to want hair, clothes, makeup to be identical to whoever's making it to the cover of *Seventeen* magazine. Normal for teenagers, that is. When we allow our *preteens* to mimic Paris Hilton and Lindsey Lohan, we've got a problem. ('Course, if we let our *teenage* girls model themselves after that crowd, we've got a problem too.) Teenage girls are almost ready for makeup and fashion anyway. Tweens aren't, unless somebody tells them they should be. High schoolers do it with an eye toward their own individuality because they recognize its importance. Elementary and middle schoolers don't have enough of a sense of themselves yet to see that. Wanting to dress like Hannah Montana is one thing; she's close to their age. But even Hannah is growing up fast—and she's "perfect." Trying to emulate somebody "perfect" is a definite barrier to discovering your tween's own wonderfully imperfect self.

The need to belong. Ever since the telephone became commonplace in the American home, tween girls have been calling each other to find out what they're wearing that day, right down to the hair barrettes. As men, we don't get that unless we compare it to wanting the right baseball mitt or skateboard when we were kids so we'd be considered cool. One of the most important issues in tweenhood is fitting in, learning how to belong to a group outside the family, where people don't necessarily have to love you. The happiness of every human being actually depends on that to a large degree. Even Jesus said, "Love one another. As I have loved you" (John 13:34), rather than, "Go out and be a rugged individualist and don't worry about being part of a community." Dude, he traveled with one. A girl between eight and twelve finds that sense of belonging by "matching" what the girls she likes are doing, whether it's in what she wears

Mini-Women

I wish my dad would understand that I am growing up. I AM! I CAN cross the street alone. I really am growing up!

or what activities she chooses or even how she talks. Hang out with your daughter and her BFFs for fifteen minutes; if you understand 50 percent of what they're saying, you're doing good.

There is absolutely nothing wrong with that. It's actually healthy. But it also creates a natural tension between wanting to belong and wanting to be a unique individual. Both are necessary and will come together at some point in her life (that's the idea, anyway!), but right now the need to be like everybody else can throw the thing off balance, especially if the other kids in her life are particularly rough on anybody who dares color outside the lines. That becomes more of an issue in middle school—ages eleven and twelve—but even younger girls are subject to ridicule if their headband is yesterday or they admit they still play with their American Girl dolls. Sometimes they find it easier to become clones than stand up for their right to be exactly who they are. Girls with low self-esteem—a weak concept of who they are—are more likely to lower their standards to please other people.

Anything that makes her "different." If you've ever had your leg in a cast or had laryngitis or anything that temporarily handicapped you, think back to how it affected you when people stared or talked unnecessarily loud at you or avoided eye contact. Most of us feel at least a little awkward, a little self-conscious in a situation like that—and we're adults. Put that on a tween girl and stick her in a classroom full of kids who have no highly developed social skills or impulse control and imagine how it feels. If your tween daughter has a physical challenge, a behavioral issue like ADHD, or a noticeable "abnormality" in her appearance (your dad's protruding ears, your out-of-control curls which she can't remedy with a buzz cut), she's a prime candidate for teasing, and, as a result, for hiding some part of herself, even from herself. It may be that this particular "flaw" never fazed her before, but don't be surprised if she's suddenly painfully aware of how it sets her apart.

And it isn't just the obvious anomalies that can put a girl in that fix. The list of "differences" is practically endless:

Being exceptionally bright.
Having some learning challenges.

Mini-Women

When I was a tween, my dad knew I was a little bit weird. I still had imaginary friends in the fifth grade! I thought I was Anne of Green Gables and dressed up in fairy princess costumes. I think it was pretty obvious back then that I wasn't quite a "normal" child.

Being, shall we say, eccentric.

Being extremely shy.

Developing sooner than the other girls.

No sign of the development the other girls are showing.

Behaving in a far more mature way than the other kids.

Being "way immature" compared to the rest of the group.

Having deep religious convictions.

Having less conservative religious beliefs than her peers.

Having an interest or hobby that isn't considered cool.

Not participating in the activity that *is* considered cool.

Being "too tall."

Being "too short."

Too round.

Too scrawny.

My dad doesn't inter-fere with who I am. I just don't think he exactly **knows** *who I am.*

You get the idea. If she isn't walking that fine line between "safely like the rest of us" and "weird," somebody's probably going to have something to say about it, and that's going to impact her being able to relax and find herself. If a nickname gets attached to that "mal-ady"—Amazon Girl, Brain Child, Geek—she's hard put to get out from under that label. She even starts to wonder, "Is that all I am?"

What "a girl" really is. Yeah, women have been liberated since about 1969, but tell that to the tween girl who stops raising her hand in class because some absurd little creep calls her a Brainiac. Or the one whose brother rolls his eyes at her (yeah, boys do it too) and tells her cheerleading isn't a sport. Or the one who hears the class bully call her a "lesbo" because she's the soccer team's star player. As a soci-ety, we still tend to assume boys will be better at math and science, girls at literature, history, and the arts. That all female children like the girly thing. That expressions of emotion from any woman past puberty can be attributed to her menstrual cycle. Don't get me wrong, there are important differences between men and women that we ignore at our peril. But it's the ones that aren't really there that affect our daughters. If yours stifles her academic, athletic, or leadership ability because she's a girl, she's giving up a valuable piece of herself. Trust me, it still happens.

And then there's you, Dad. Without even knowing it, you can make it harder for your daughter to embrace who she was made to be. You don't do it on purpose. You don't do it consciously. Maybe you don't do it at all. But because you still have such a powerful influence on her, your reaction to who she is truly becoming can send any part of that skittering under the rug—or bring it out where she can love it. It's not all on you, obviously, but you do play a major role. All of the following have an effect on who she thinks she is:

How much you talk to her—and how you talk to her—and how much you listen to her.

How much time you spend doing things with her.

How much interest you take in her schooling—how involved you are in her activities—how aware you are of her life outside the family.

How you react to new developments in her personality.

Whether you like her—whether you have expectations of who she's going to be.

With all that waiting in front of her like hurdles in the 400, how does any little girl ever grow up with a strong sense of herself? That's where we're taking you next.

In Reality

You can't help your daughter be herself if you don't know who she is. Mark all the following things that you know about your tween daughter:

○ her fave color
○ what kind of music she likes
○ her preferred pizza toppings
○ which books she's read over and over
○ who she looks up to
○ her biggest fear
○ what she wants to be when she grows up (as of this week)
○ her highest hope

Mini-Women

I wish my dad would understand that I am different from him. Sometimes I really don't think he gets that.

- ○ the thing that makes her the most angry
- ○ her mental picture of God

If you marked none or very few, don't feel like a loser dad. So you've got some research to do. Take your daughter out for ice cream and start asking. Even if you checked all or most, it would be a good idea to run this past her anyway. Should it turn out your answers are right, sweet. You've been paying attention. And in the event that what you thought you knew is, well, wrong, your daughter will enjoy correcting you. Have that conversation over a slice of pizza. While you're at it, you might come up with some questions of your own.

One more thing. Listen to what she says about *you*. Are you often told you're the best dad in the galaxy? Or are you hearing that you're always too busy? That you're no fun? That you're always criticizing? Consider the fact that it might just be true.

Learning from the Master

The Gospels are full of references to denying your false self, finding your true self through service, being genuinely humble about who you really are. Jesus gives us a total textbook on authenticity. But the passage that really nails it is this one:

> *Whoever did want him,*
> *who believed he was who he claimed*
> *and would do what he said,*
> *He made to be their true selves,*
> *their child-of-God selves.*
>
> John 1:12 – 13, *The Message*

Those two verses say several things that are essential for dads raising daughters.

One: becoming who she was made to be is *the* God-established goal of her life. It all comes down to that, to discovering her true self and embracing it and living into it. John doesn't say, "Whoever believes will be made to follow certain rules, espouse a particular doctrine, belong to a prescribed political party." The first thing after

"Want him, believed [in him], do what he said," is "[you'll be] made to be [your] true self." Which leads us to—

Two: she doesn't have to create a self or invent somebody to be. Christ will give her the freedom to be what she already is, made by God as his child. Even the discovering of self isn't all that hard because in her relationship with him, she's going to be shown what's there in ways she isn't even conscious of most of the time.

So, three: it's pointless—godless, actually—for you to decide who you want her to be, tell her what that is, and shove her toward it. Dude, it's in there. She's going to do the discovering. All you have to do is help her find her connection with God and give her opportunities to experience what she's learning from him.

Yeah, that's all.

Okay, it's a lot. But it's a God-thing, something you really can't blow off. *You'll* get guidance too. So start praying.

Where Do I Come In?

We're referring to this area as "authenticity." Some people call it "self-image" or "self-esteem" or "self-confidence." Whatever you name it, right now, in her tween years, this finding of self so she can be all she was meant to be is fragile. As we've already pointed out, the barriers to authenticity she faces every day can make her feel like an eggshell. You are, unfortunately, like the king's men who can't put Humpty Dumpty together again every time she falls. Nor can you remove every barrier so that she never falls at all. What you *can* do is help her strengthen that fragile shell of identity so that it doesn't shatter so easily, *and* you can make certain that you aren't one of the barriers yourself. We've identified some things that may help you achieve both.

Give her special attention. You've heard this before: few fathers ever die wishing they had spent more time at the office. We aren't going to beat that dead horse. You have to make a living. The major thing you do is provide for your family. And these days, if you're going to do that, you have to be there first and stay the longest and work the hardest. Which means there's not much left of you when

Mini-Women

When I was a tween, my dad didn't REALLY, REALLY, REALLY know who I was. It might have been because he was very busy at work.

My dad and I go on "Daddy Daughter Dates." He normally just takes me to the bookstore or we go out for ice cream and talk about what's been going on in our lives recently. He works really hard at knowing how I'm doing and what I'm having trouble with, even if he does get a little forgetful at times.

you get home, and there's always stuff that has to get done there, especially if your wife works too. Not so much with the slippers and the mail waiting by your chair while she fixes supper and keeps the children away from you until you've watched the news.

We get that in the face of all that, it's hard to really focus on your daughter. And we're not saying that from the minute you walk in the door after work until she goes to bed, you have to devote yourself entirely to tween issues. You do actually have to remain sane — you still have the teen years ahead, after all. There are several balanced things you can do, though, that will meet her need for attention from you.

Schedule regular times to be with just her. If you've got other kids, you travel a lot, you're heavily involved in church work in addition to your job, she can be easily lost in the proverbial shuffle. A lot of girls this age won't say, "Hey, what about me?" They'll just assume they're not important enough to be squeezed into your schedule. Unlike boys, who are much more likely to make their wishes known. Loudly and with a side of obnoxia.

The solution to that is to make one evening a month, or every two weeks, or once a week Dad-and-daughter time. I didn't do this. Wish I had. Dads who do say it's a highlight, and that they don't get any less done because they're spending an hour or two a week with a daughter. These "regular appointments" range from picking a daughter up

My dad is a GREAT dad and I love him a bunch. It's just that a lot of times, I feel like he doesn't have time for me so he doesn't understand me.

I don't think my dad really knows who I am. He seems to spend a lot more time and money on my brothers, which, to be honest, makes me kind of jealous, even though I know I shouldn't be.

from dance class Tuesday nights and hitting Baskin-Robbins on the way home to monthly "Daddy Daughter Dates" that include dinner at Wendy's or a visit to Petsmart to check out the cats that are up for adoption. A girl understands tough economic times and is usually just as thrilled with a weekly game of Monopoly or the two of you watching reruns of the *Cosby Show* as she is with Miley Cyrus tickets, as long as she can count on that time being as important to you as it is to her. I do remember regular *Star Wars* movie marathons where Marijean and I shared several bags of microwave popcorn and recited the dialogue together. Wish I'd done that more. Don't end up wishing. Just do it.

Let her pick the activity sometimes. You might be thinking you have to come up with all these creative ideas that require you somehow knowing what she's going to enjoy doing. The whole point of this is for her to not only know she's special but to find out just what it is that's special about her. Put a time and cost limit on it and see what she comes up with. You might be surprised when she says, "Let's go to the bookstore and I'll show you what I like and you show me what you like." Who knew she'd be jazzed about trying take-out sushi, or learning to play horseshoes, or watching a chef toss pizza dough (and then taking a pie home)? You-pick-this-time-I'll-choose-next-time works too. You never know what she might find out about herself while she's fishing or playing a computer game or watching a basketball game with you. She wants you in her world, but she also wants to be in yours.

Share a hobby. Before you think "Look, I'm not going to collect stickers with the kid," think outside the box. This doesn't have to be a major deal. Just be on the lookout for any interest you and she have in common. You both dig *Animal Planet*? Turn her on to some good animal websites. Observe the squirrels in the backyard while you're sharing Saturday breakfast. Let her help you pick out the bird feeders and get her to read up on which species eat what. Are you both into the incredible things computers can do? Both drawn to classical music (or country or contemporary Christian)? Can't get enough of soccer or gardening or reading about the Civil War and neither can she? See what you can do to bring her in with you, even on a small

> ### Mini-Women
>
> *I am always myself around my dad. I feel comfortable around him and he loves me for who I am. I mean, I AM his daughter.*

scale. Not only are you spending time with her, which raises her self-esteem, but you're encouraging her to pursue the things that get her individual juices flowing, rather than just what all the other kids are doing (i.e., parking in front of the TV or texting each other).

Teach her things that will make her feel confident and independent. How to change a tire, mow the lawn, know one Harley from another (you never know when that might come up). Marijean wanted to know how an engine works. I taught her how to make great gravy. The daughter of a buddy of mine wanted to help when they went out on their boat, so he took her to boating school. Not only was she the youngest, but she scored the highest and can dock a vessel better than most of the weekenders on the water. Another friend who's raising his daughter on his own showed her at ten how to balance a checkbook and stay on budget buying school clothes. A lot of guys wish their wives had had that kind of training. The more tween girls know how to do, the more sure of themselves they'll be—and that makes them less likely to believe it when some kid says they're dumb or stupid or lame. No girl who can change the oil in her dad's truck is going to be easily put down by some boy who doesn't even seem to know his correct pants size.

Show an interest in the life she has outside the family. This is both an awesome and a scary time for your tween daughter, because she's making her first forays out into the world where people don't *have* to embrace her the way they do at home. In fact, they can take her or leave her, so her school life, her extracurricular activities, and her church involvement are really forums for her to discover what works for her and what doesn't in terms of fitting in. All the feedback she gets out there isn't going to be positive and, in fact, it can be down-right hurtful. Rather than giving in to the urge to punch out anybody who bruises your baby's feelings, you'll do better to get acquainted with how she spends her time when she isn't at home and let her know you're behind her.

Some dads totally get into that. A friend of ours who has triplet daughters (yeah, you think you've got challenges …) has immersed himself in their soccer world. He coaches the team, travels with them, and helps raise money for them to participate in tournaments. Those girls know Dad is on their side, and it shows in their relationship with him. Not every dad can do that, nor would you probably want to if your daughter's on the dance team or is running her own poetry-writing club (this week). Sometimes just asking how it's going on a regular basis, and actually listening to the answer, is enough. And giving concrete support when you can. One dad we know cooks burgers and dogs for his daughter's dance team fund-raisers. Another one—a single dad—makes sure his daughter never misses her art class even when he's dog tired. One attorney dad in Marijean's elementary school days arranged his schedule so he could chaperone field trips.

One thing that it's essential you do is to be aware of what's going on with your tween academically and to be part of her support whenever possible. While Nancy did most of the day-to-day homework supervising, I got into helping Marijean with science projects and presentations that required hands on. She even took me to school as part of her report on the Navy SEALS in seventh grade. Talk about your visual aids.

Dads are often given the task of helping their girl children with the "guy" subjects like math and science. The more literary guys are called on to give a hand with language arts and anything requiring writing. Great, except that (a) you may be an algebra whiz but not be able to explain simple math facts to your daughter and (b) it may come so easily to you that you get impatient with her inability to "get it." The opportunities for making her feel like a complete moron are endless in these situations. So—remember that she isn't you. That her natural aptitude, or lack of it, only makes her slower to catch on; it doesn't make her a hopeless case. That praise and patience are everything. Her frustration may lead to whining, crying, and collapsing facedown on the dining room table. Take a break, regroup, come back to it. Keep your sense of humor even when she loses hers. And try to avoid saying the following:

Don't Say It, Dude ...

"You're just not trying hard enough."
"Are you even listening to me?"

My dad has always encouraged me to be myself and to excel in my hobbies. Some things that are "me," like bright colors of nail polish and purple eyeshadow, he doesn't understand, but for the most part he always encourages me to be me.

My dad is normally busy with his work during the day, so he isn't really that much involved in my home schooling. But he tries his best to help out when I'm struggling in math or when I'm presenting a report.

My dad seemed to like my brother and sister better because they could play soccer. I tried to be good at soccer just so he would like me better too. But he talked to me about it and told me I was special and that I didn't have to play if I didn't want to. Now he helps me be the best artist I can be.

I don't think my dad would want to make me someone who isn't me.

"Come on, it's not that hard."

"What's your problem? I could do this in third grade."

"All right, sit up and concentrate."

"You've already made up your mind that you can't do this, so I can't help you."

"I've explained it every way I know how. You must have a mental block."

"I'm obviously not the one to teach you this. Where's your mother?"

Avoid pushing her into activities she doesn't like just because you think they'll be good for her. Sports come immediately to mind. While participation in team athletics has all kinds of benefits, not every tween girl is ready for and interested in playing organized soccer or trying out for the softball team. She may not even be physically suited for it. If every adult woman doesn't play tennis or participate on the church volleyball team, why should every mini-woman? Put her out there on a field or court where she feels inadequate, inept, and completely uncoordinated, and she is not going to experience any of the benefits sports are supposed to provide for her. In fact, the exact opposite is likely to happen, and instead of helping her gain confidence in who she is, you've merely pointed out to her what she isn't.

If your daughter does enjoy participating in sports, let her enjoy it. She's a kid. She'll still be a kid when she's a teenager. A kid doesn't need to have her every move dissected when she's out there having a good time and learning about teamwork and healthy competition. If you're doing it because you plan on her getting an athletic scholarship to college, you might want to rethink that. Only about 5 percent of high school athletes continue to play competitively in college, and no more than 1 percent get full scholarships.[1] If she's the one who has her heart set on that, leave the coaching to her coach and concentrate on making sure she's healthy and balanced and encouraged. Don't make riding home with you after games and practices the worst part of her day.

All of the above applies to any activity you're "making" your daughter take part in, even though she'd rather undergo torture, just because you think it would do her good. Whether it's playing a musical instrument, taking dance lessons, or being in the Girl Scouts—whatever it is, it will do her more harm than good if while she's doing it she feels like she can't measure up or constantly gets the sense that she's a failure. This stuff is supposed to be fun. If you want her to have experience with a lot of different things so she can discover what she likes, let her choose what those things are. Sure, put limits on the number and establish how long she needs to stick with something before she decides it isn't for her. Know that she's probably not going to discover her lifetime passion at ten. It's normal for her to sample what's on the buffet table. Just don't load up her plate for her.

Give her meaningful chores so she can be a part of the running of the household. In addition to having her keep her room tidy (or some facsimile thereof) and generally picking up after herself, make sure she's involved in tasks that put her beside you and the rest of the family. A field day for yard cleanup. A weekly meal where everybody has a part in getting it on the table. Cleaning out the garage or attic as a group. I tended to be pretty much "Look, I just want to get this done, so go play," which I know now was a mistake. But one thing I did include Marijean in was washing the cars. She did that with me from the time she was a toddler, and even when she was in college, she wanted to go with me to the car wash when she was home on break. Since Nancy equates going to the grocery store with having a root canal, Mj and I also did a lot of food shopping together. Yeah, there are some tasks you have to do on your own and you get them done a lot faster if you don't have all your offspring tagging along behind you. But if there are some that can involve your daughter, she'll not only have that extra time with you that she craves but she'll find out she's capable and she'll have more of a sense of ownership in the household (and will be less likely to trash the place).

Remove as many Tease Targets as you can. Kids this age tease. Especially boys. It's like it's in their contract. Yet no matter how much of it our daughters hear—or dish out—when it's directed at them, it goes straight to their self-esteem and leaves a mark. We've already talked about how you can curb your own teasing, but you can also help your daughter keep her still-delicate sense of herself intact by

My dad thinks I can't handle ANYTHING. I want to help out around the house, but he thinks I can't do it because I'm too little.

In the morning when I just roll out of bed, my dad's all like "Wake up, love. The sun came to see you." I love that.

*I wish my dad would
care more when I'm
talking. Like if I'm telling
him something that
happened at school, he
doesn't seem that in-
terested. I love my dad
and he is soooo nice,
but I wish he listened to
me more.*

*Okay, the dad problem:
He never listens to me.
He doesn't understand
that I need him to, so
sometimes I just don't
tell him about what I
really feel.*

doing away with some of the things that make her a walking bull's eye for taunting. A few examples:

If she's being teased for having "man legs" because the hormones have kicked in and made them mega-hairy, let her shave her legs, for Pete's sake. Her mother may protest, "Once you start doing it you have to keep doing it," but I've never had the shaving police come to the door and enforce that "rule." If she needs relief now, what's the big deal?

If she's being called a freak because she still has a Beauty and the Beast backpack—which is in perfectly good shape—remember that in her world, the material items are signals used to craft an identity with the group. To be too far out of it can potentially place her in freak terri-tory.[2] Backpacks aren't that expensive. You're not sending the message that if she has the right things she'll be accepted. You're just sparing her unnecessary embarrassment until everybody grows up.

If she has any of the aforementioned "differences" that are draw-ing cruel treatment, talk to her about the methods for handling that which we'll discuss in the next chapter, under bullying. If she's really self-conscious, help her find ways to make it a cool part of who she is. Get her the trendiest glasses they make. Let her go for the colored braces or the transparent ones. But don't just tell her nobody notices and not to worry about it. They do, and she will, unless you help her.

Give plenty of positive feedback. Tween girls need twice the posi-tive feedback you think they do. That doesn't mean you have to be gushing over her like Old Faithful 24/7. But when you do see some-thing in her that rocks, you aren't going to make her vain by telling her so. Where did that line of thinking come from anyway? Girls will live up to whoever you think they are. If they know you think they're smart, witty, responsible, compassionate, and interesting, that's what they'll continue to be. And the only way they're going to know you think that is if you tell them. Keep it genuine, as we've mentioned before, and your daughter will flourish under your compliments about her child-of-God qualities:

Her sense of humor.

Her basic nature (energetic, dreamy, competitive, compassionate, wacky-in-a-good-way).

The way she treats her friends, her mom, her siblings, you.
Her strengths.
The things she's improving on.
How she's reflecting her relationship with God.

Praise her for her accomplishments too and, again, let her know you think she's beautiful. Just put more emphasis on who she is than what she does or what she looks like or what she owns.

Negative feedback, on the other hand, is about the worst thing you can lay on your daughter in her tween years. That doesn't mean don't correct her, don't discipline her, don't call her on it when she acts out. We're talking about attacks on who she is:

Don't Say It, Dude …

"You're as bad as your mother."
"See, that's what I don't like about you."
"I don't like you when you act like that."
"You're a bad sport …"
"… a couch potato."
"You're dense …"
"… bossy …"
"… too emotional."
"I don't know why you have to be like that."

If she makes herself and everyone around her unhappy, find out why. But don't assume that's her basic personality and criticize her for it. Harsh judgment never made anybody a better person.

Listen to her. Really listen. We've mentioned this before, but it bears repeating (even for guys who hate to be told twice). I know she can probably talk longer than you can listen to her. I had one of those. Still do. But when she's on a roll, either tune in and respond with something beyond "That's great, honey. All right" or make a date for a good talk. However, a lot of the really important stuff that comes out of her mouth is going to be a spontaneous, one-time-only thing. If you know you've missed about half of what she's said to you since she learned to talk, try listening to everything in a single

My dad thinks my mom is stupid heaps of times, and the same with me. I really want him to NOT think we're dumb.

My dad doesn't know who I really am because he only asks me questions that will mean nothing the next day. Things like "How'd your day go?" Nothing else. I don't think he really wants to hear what I have to say.

I change my mind pretty often about what I want to be when I grow up, but my dad listens to every one, encourages me, tells me what he thinks, and gives me a chance to grow where I want to grow.

My daddy knows me … but not who I am way, way deep down. Just half the way down.

sitting and sort out what was just a matter of having your attention and taking full advantage of it, and what actually told you something about her. With some practice, you'll be able to do some "Uh-uh. No kidding?" listening, but perk up your ears when she comes out with something like "Is it okay for me to have a boyfriend?"

If she's not much of a talker (are you sure this child's female?), ask her questions you know she can warm up to. Specific questions. If you're at a loss, refer to "In Reality," pages 93–94. Girls love that kind of stuff. Nancy's never missed yet with "If you were a car (animal, fruit, brand of shoe), what do you think you'd be?" as a conversation starter with tweens. Tween girls love to play, and they are the most themselves when they do.

Basically, make her feel important as often as you can, because she may not feel that way anywhere else in that world she's trying to navigate. It's on you to show her what it's like to feel special. She's not going to completely know who she is, much less be that absolutely all the time until — well, it's a lifelong process. Nor are you going to know everything there is to know about her. That's part of the mystery of being a woman. But your power as a father is to see that she has every chance to get started on that journey and that she has all the support she needs as she ventures out. It may be the only power you really have.

Bridging the Gap

Father, I know you want my girl-child to be the person you created her to be. Please bridge the gap between what she needs to discover and my ability to open the doors for her. Can't do it without you. Counting on you, Father.

Amen.

6

Dealing with Girl Drama

What Just Happened?

You pull into the parking lot of the dance studio and look for your daughter in the knot of tweenies just inside the glass doors. She'll be the one at the center of it, coordinating who's going to call who at what time because clearly, in the nine hours they've already spent together today, they haven't gotten to say everything that needs to be said. Whoever estimated that a man speaks 10,000 words a day, while a woman utters 30,000, was only talking about adults. In your experience, a mini-woman speaks at least 50,000, and at the exact same time as all her friends. Your daughter will probably speak another thousand before she sees that you're waiting.

You peer through the windshield and try to pick her out of the myriad of tossing ponytails. But she's not in that pink huddle. She's off to the side with just one of the girls you're pretty sure has passed through your home at some point. Their conversation has the look of a summit conference—shoulders conspiratorially hunched, eyes eating each other's faces, teeth clenched so that the words have to squeeze out between the cracks. Something heavy is going down.

Even as your daughter catches your eye and heads for the door, you're flipping through the possible scenarios. Somebody got the wrong color tutu. No, judging from the pinched-in look on your daughter's face as she approaches the car, it's worse than that. Somebody got kicked out of the class. *She* got kicked out of the class. You always thought that teacher was a whack job.

Mini-Women

If I brought home five of my friends and asked my dad to name them . . . he would probably be clueless.

You start to turn off the engine, ready to go in there and set this woman straight. But your daughter climbs into the car, heaves her bag onto the floor, and fastens her seatbelt like she's strapping on a holster for the showdown.

"What's wrong?" you say.

"Nothing," she says.

"Now, clearly, *something* is wrong—"

"I don't want to talk about it," she says.

Now there's a new twist. Not sure exactly what to do with that, you pull out of the parking lot, eyes darting periodically to the rear-view mirror, where you can see her fuming. If you're not mistaken, steam is surging from her flared nostrils. Maybe you don't want to know after all.

"Okay," you say, "if you don't want to talk, I'm not going to push—"

"I am so mad at her!"

So you were right. Score one for the dad.

"Your teacher," you say.

You get a blank look in the rearview. "Why would I be mad at her?" Oh.

"I'm mad at—" She utters the name of one of the girls in the knot she wasn't standing in.

"What did she do?" you ask. And then you immediately know that was a mistake. Steam now spews from her ears as well, and she wriggles herself up onto her knees.

"Okay," she says, "so I'm like just talking to one of my other friends—you know—"

Another name comes out. You nod, even though you couldn't pick that person out of a lineup.

"—and it wasn't like I was all shutting her out, but that's what she thought so she goes and tells—"

Yet another name somebody's mother made up.

"So then I try to explain to her that it was like no big deal, but she just turns her back on me, and so I'm like, okay, fine, be that way. And it was, like, over, but then Ms.—"

"That's the teacher," you say, in an attempt to make some sense out of all this.

Huge sigh. "No, Dad, that's the *assistant*."

"Sorry," you say, "my bad."

"She gets in my face for not focusing, but how am I supposed to do that when now everybody's mad at me?"

You don't ask how "everybody" got involved. It's complicated enough as it is. Your job is to un-complicate it before the child implodes in the back seat.

"Sounds like" — you search for the girl's name but it escapes you — "she's got issues. You just need to drop that chick and stick with your other friends."

"Da-ad!" she says. "I can't!"

"If she treats you that way, why not?"

She slides forward as far as the seatbelt will allow. "Because," she says, "she's my best friend."

You don't reply. You still have about five hundred words left in your day, but you know none of them are going to be right.

———

There is probably no tween girl issue where dads are more clue-less than in the arena of girl politics. You can understand hormones better than you can best friend complexities and clique hierarchy, because at least there's some scientific basis for body chemistry. The minute you think you get the girl drama, it all explodes in your face and somebody's running off to the bathroom crying with an entou-rage behind her.

It truly is a girl thing, so don't think you're ever going to under-stand it entirely. We can give you some basics, though, that will keep you from putting your foot in it with your daughter and help you guide her when even she doesn't understand it. Before you wimp out and make this her mother's sole responsibility, remember that rela-tionships are everything to a woman, no matter what her age. It's in her DNA to have them, nurture them, and thrive within them. If you decide to remain completely uninvolved, you're making a choice not to help shape the foundation of her life. That doesn't make it much of a choice. We're not going to try to get you to referee whatever's going on in that bathroom where somebody's crying. We just think some insights might help you both.

Here's the Deal

Nobody can lay out for you exactly what's going to happen as your daughter forms relationships in her tween years because, frankly, it's too complex. To try to make it at least somewhat clear, we've sorted the thing into five parts. If you have some clarity in each one, you won't find yourself asking the question sure to win you total contempt: *Why can't you all just get along?*

#1. Why this is so important to her

This is the way Nancy describes tween girl relationships in *Mom's Ultimate Guide to the Tween Girl World*, and we think it bears repeating here, since it highlights the differences between daughters and sons.

"Standing on an intermediate school playground during recess is an education in itself.

"The tween boys bolt out of the building already yelling—about what, no one knows—and immediately become involved in some activity that involves throwing something, climbing on something, jumping from something, or concocting something. Punching each other for no apparent reason will also be part of that. If they stop moving and start talking, it's either to plan the next throwing-climbing-jumping-concocting-punching thing, or to agree on how to get the most squealing out of the girls with their throwing-climbing-jumping-etc. Tween boys can be so wonderfully predictable. Seriously. If a disagreement arises, they solve it with a shove or a shout, and five minutes later (if it even takes that long) they're back to throwing-climbing-jumping as if nothing ever happened.

"And then you have the tween girls.

"A trifle more sedate than the boys at this age, they stroll out of the building, sometimes arm in arm, already chattering—about what, *everyone* knows because they do it non-stop, whether you want to hear it or not—and immediately busy themselves with getting into groups. One group settles against the fence. Another gathers around the playground equipment that nobody actually plays on anymore because that would not be cool. Still another hangs out by the water fountain, because the boys all end up needing a drink of water at some point after all that throwing-climbing-jumping-concocting-and-punching, and even though they're absurd little creeps, there's something fascinating about them. A few girls don't seem to have a group, but rather than band together and form their own, they wander wistfully at the fringes of the others, some quite obviously longing to be invited in, others pretending, just as obviously, that they don't care that they're alone.

"Once the groups have been established, some activities might begin. That group gets up a game of jump rope or practices cheers. That one sits in a circle and does … something that periodically makes them erupt into shrieks. And that group by the water fountain spends the period rolling eyes and flipping hair and hoping some boy will reveal something about the boy-world that they can write notes to each other about for the rest of the day.

"When the bell rings, they all return to class, boys and girls, to practice long division and use vocabulary words in a sentence. But one of the most important parts of their education has already taken place out there among the swings and the slides.

"The boys are learning how to stand out, prove themselves, become independent and still be okay in the group—because who are you going to throw-climb-jump-concoct-and-punch with if you don't have friends?

"The girls are learning to connect, give and take, care and be cared for—because how will you know who you are and how to behave if you don't have friends? Close friends. *Best* friends."[1]

So it's just part of being a girl? Really?

Really. Gender studies of preschool toy preference (where they get the ideas for these studies no one knows) showed that three- to four-year-old girls choose the telephone as their favorite toy more often than boys.[2] That tendency to make communicating with friends the

> **Mini-Women**
>
> *One thing I wish my dad knew is that us girls need a lot of time together by ourselves. I mean, like, a LOT of time.*

center of their universe increases when they hit puberty because of hormones. No lie. Estrogen and progesterone basically make females create, be aware of the big picture, communicate, and be in relationship.[3] Who knew?

Then there's a girl's natural psychological development. Even if she's an introvert, at this stage in her life she becomes less separate and defines herself largely by how she connects with other girls her own age. If who she's discovering herself to be is okay in her girl world, her confidence soars. If it isn't, she either looks for ways to be herself among her peers without ridicule or exclusion, or she puts on a false self that works. You can see how vital it is that she have same-age relationships that allow her to be genuine as she grows into her identity. No wonder the world revolves around her BFFs. They are her lifelines to herself.

A whole lot goes on there too besides giggling and talking ninety miles an hour. In her relationships with her friends and her dealings with the not-so-much friends, your daughter is learning major life skills. This is where she figures out how to get along with people who don't *have* to love her, how to handle conflict, how to trust and be trusted—the list goes on. This is huge stuff in the making of a young woman.

#2. What normal tween-girl friendships look like

Although it may not look "normal" to you, these are the kinds of things that typically go on among tween girls who are friends:

Giggling together until they can't breathe (don't call 911).
Finishing each other's sentences (not the same as interrupting, just so you know).
Appearing to have a language of their own (they're not speaking code to keep things from you).
Whispering behind closed doors (they are not gearing up for a coup in there).
Passionately defending each other (on things that seem pretty trivial to you).
Being totally themselves with each other (even if they're awkward with everybody else).

Mini-Women

One thing I wish my dad would get is that girls love to just hang out and spend time with friends for no apparent reason. Is that okay?

Other normal friendship occurrences may seem sort of negative to you, but there's no need to get worked up about any of that, either, because it's all part of the learning curve in a girl group:

Somebody gets left out once in a while (usually accidentally).

Friendships end without drama (somebody moves, they realize they were only friends because their mothers were, that kind of thing).

They fight and "break up" and become friends again (sometimes all in the same day ... or hour).

Somebody's feelings get hurt (like when teasing can't be erased with "Just kidding").

They get irritated with each other (especially if they've spent a big block of time stuck together like strips of Velcro).

Those rough spots usually result in a brief flare-up, followed by a return to the status quo. Congress could take lessons from tween girls when it comes to repairing differences and moving on.

#3. What's cause for concern in a friendship

Compared to adults, tween girls are still pretty immature socially—which is why they have to spend so much time practicing. That, coupled with the fact that their relationships with other girls are so intense and so important to them, makes for a fair amount of the drama you may be seeing at home. This is the kind of thing that sends a daughter crying to her room:

Mean-spirited, behind-the-back gossip (a time-honored female tradition).

Lies and rumors (and the juicier the better).

Betrayals of confidence (i.e., those secret whispers you heard? They're now being whispered outside the closed doors).

One girl in the friendship trying to control the whole show (not to be confused with leadership).

Jealousy (of what "she" has, of the attention "she" gets, of the friends "she" has "stolen").

Teasing that gets out of hand (being mean is evidently the new confident).

Deliberate exclusion and shunning (as well-planned as a corporate takeover).

Possessiveness (along the lines of "If you invite her to eat at our table, you're not my friend anymore.").

Constant drama (of soap opera proportions).

When girls get involved in that, they aren't displaying some inherent mean streak. They just aren't very good at relationships yet, and they're providing the adults in their lives with some teachable moments. More on that later in the chapter. For now, just know that (a) it isn't okay behavior and needs to be corrected, and (b) it isn't a sign that your daughter is evil in her soul.

#4. What a "clique" looks like

It's healthy for a tween girl to have a gaggle of three to five girls who are together because they share common interests—beyond what they own and what their daddies do to support that. They're open to new friends, and there aren't any "requirements" for being in the group except being themselves and letting everybody else be their authentic selves too. Notwithstanding the occasional spat—or even a temporary dip into the challenges we listed above—a healthy circle of girlfriends should make your daughter's social life delightful and secure and brimming with giggles.

What sometimes happens, though, is that a knot of three or four of them glom together because the leader decides that's the way it's going to be, a.k.a. the Queen Bee (so named by author Rosalind Wiseman in her book *Queen Bees and Wannabees*).[4] This girl decides who gets in and who goes out, the former being based on where a girl lives, what she wears, and what she possesses. The QB also recognizes what roles various girls can play in keeping her at the top and establishes a hierarchy, even in elementary school. (Tina Fey's movie *Mean Girls* is based on Wiseman's book; while a little over the top, it's still a disturbingly true picture of what goes on.) We're talking about a clique here, and if a tween is in one, she has to work hard to stay there because membership is subject to change at the whim of the Queen.[5] Being an individual isn't encouraged; a girl simply bases her worth on whether she's accepted by the clique.

Your daughter may refer to such a group as The Popular Girls (which may expand to include boys in middle school and be renamed The Popular *Kids*). This is not to be confused with girls who are popular because everyone likes them for their great personalities and the kind, open way they treat other people. A "popular clique" is made up of girls who like power. Theirs is a group other girls may want to get into because it not only raises their status but provides them with protection from that capricious control.

Just because the girls in your daughter's little posse all talk alike, dress alike, and spontaneously shriek at the same unprovoked moment doesn't mean she has a clique going. Some "group think" is healthy—the same taste in music, the same opinion of boys, the same slang. That's part of the fun of belonging. But if she can't express any deviation from what the group thinks for fear of being excluded from the lunch table and the next exodus to the bathroom, that's a problem.

#5. What bullying looks like

Clique behavior borders on disturbing, but we're not even at full-blown ugly yet, not until we talk about the vicious, mean, calculating, deliberate takedown perpetrated by the girl bully. As a guy you may need to reroute your thinking here.

When you remember bullying, what comes to mind is probably the big tough kid who beat you up for your lunch money, or the gang of big-tough-kid-plus-cronies who threw skinny guys out of the locker room naked or stuffed them into the school trash cans. A bully girl's weapon of choice is usually something verbal. With the rise of physical aggression among girls, some take up male tactics and throw punches and pull hair. But a Really Mean Girl (RMG) is more likely to resort to what psychologists call "relational aggression," and it applies to the tween or teen who is out to damage her victim's social standing by intentionally manipulating how other people see her. Boys hit or shove or pound. Girls isolate or exclude, spread vicious rumors, post lies online, and create situations just to humiliate their target in front of others.

Girl bullying starts to appear in about third grade, just when your daughter is entering her tween years. It intensifies during middle

Mini-Women

According to my mom, if I were a boy (and therefore interested in beating people up), my dad would teach me how to break their noses.

school because, by then, cruelty has become a habit for some girls—and it's a dangerous one. Yeah, bullying has always been around, but it is *not* "just a normal phase kids go through," and they don't "just grow out of it." Successful bullies commonly carry their intimidating behavior into their adult lives. Victims of bullying carry the scars.

That old thing about "sticks and stones may break my bones, but words will never hurt me" is basically a sack of cow manure. Taunts and malicious gossip are traumatizing to a tween girl. Relational abuse is as deeply damaging as a punch in the face because it can lead the victim straight to low self-esteem, almost unbearable sadness, anxiety, anger, and social withdrawal. It can affect a girl's academic performance and increase her risk for depression. Actual suicides have been reported as the result of long-term female bullying. Are you convinced yet that this is a serious issue?

It's a mistake to assume that bullying doesn't exist in your daughter's world just because she hasn't talked about it. Here are some statistics that may blow you away:

According to the National Education Association, bully fears prompt 160,000 kids to skip school every day.[6]

In one survey, 40 percent of fifth through eighth graders say they've been sexually harassed by their peers.[7]

In another, 25 percent of the children surveyed said bullying was a significant problem for them.[8]

Forty-five percent of the tween girls in that same study said they have been cyberbullied,[9] which is the use of any electronic device to intimidate another person. Email. Website. Facebook or MySpace. Blog. Chat room or forum. Text. Cell phone call.

You might think that since that kind of intimidation isn't done face-to-face it would be less threatening than, say, name-calling in the hall. But it can actually be more frightening.

If a girl gets a threat from an unidentified emailer to "watch her back" tomorrow during recess, she doesn't know who to watch *for*, so she sees everybody as her potential stalker and turns into a bundle of anxiety.

If she gets texts calling her every foul name known to tweendom, she goes to school not knowing who hates her, so she thinks it's everybody.

If somebody spreads a rumor about her on a blog, how's she supposed to defend herself? Hundreds of kids could've seen that. If she gets embarrassed when you tease her at the dinner table, think what *that's* going to do to her.

Besides all of that, online bullying happens in her own personal space and can be read and reread, as she would put it, a bajillion times, which cuts deeper than just hearing it once. And since it's virtually anonymous, it's safer for other girls who otherwise wouldn't have the nerve to bully to get in on it and feel powerful.

Numbers can't begin to reflect the harm done to girls involved in bullying, and here's why. An attack by a bully is seldom one drive-by hit. An RMG likes the cringing, crying, crumpling response she usually gets from her target. She wants more of that I'm-in-power feeling, so she creates an ongoing, escalating threat. Her target, on the other hand, feels increasingly power*less*. The list of possible damages looks like this:

She believes she's everything the bully says she is — in essence, a complete loser.

She's angry with herself because she can't stop this person from making her life miserable.

The result is depression. Her appetite and sleep are adversely affected. Her grades drop. She feigns illness or actually feels physically ill. The sparkle is gone from her eyes.

If the abuse turns physical, she can be injured or just lose it and start punching back. Can you blame her?

If the abuse goes on, she may start believing she deserves to be hurt and begin to hurt herself. Cutting and eating disorders such as anorexia aren't uncommon in bullying victims — even in the tween years.

Her trust in people erodes and she becomes lonely and isolated.

Her confidence in social situations dwindles to nothing, and her state of self-doubt follows her into adulthood, where she remains a potential victim for adult bullies. Including, perhaps, the man she marries.

If you're like most dads, you read all of that and you're ready to go to that school and kick some serious tail until something's done about the situation. We'll talk in depth about what to do later in the chapter. For now, let's return to the normal side of tween girl politics. (Ya gotta admit, talking about bullying makes the everyday girl drama seem like a sit com.)

In Reality

You're not privy to everything that goes on with your daughter and the other girls in her life — nor should you be. She's learning some autonomy, and that's one of the main goals in growing up.

But you *can* be aware of how her relationships are affecting her, and that doesn't require eavesdropping on the sleepover. (Trust me, you don't want to do that. In fact, you don't even want to *be* there.) You can glean a lot of what you need to know just by paying attention.

What to look for? Mark any of these statements that are, from your observations, true.

List 1

○ I see pretty much the same girl or group of girls passing through our house or hanging out with my daughter at church and other venues.

○ I hear giggling (and maybe shrieking) and lots of chatter when she and her friend(s) are together.

○ My daughter has a best friend and I know her name.

○ My daughter is invited to other girls' houses.

○ When her birthday's approaching, she wants a party with her friends.

○ She seems to have one or two close friends and appears to be fine with that.

○ She asks to bring a friend when we go on a family outing.

○ It seems like there's always somebody spending the night with her on the weekends.

○ She's cried about a friendship problem.

○ She's shown an interest in having a cell phone (if not texting privileges, her own computer, and a Facebook page).

Mini-Women

Certain events recently occurred that dampened my trust in the people I called friends. I dealt with it by shoving everyone away, including my parents, whom I had a good relationship with before. My father couldn't help me because he didn't understand what was going on.

List 2

○ I can't keep track of her friends because they always seem to be different.

○ Some of her friends make plans with her and cancel at the last minute — on a regular basis.

○ When I see her with her friends, she always seems to be a few steps behind.

○ She changes BFFs often (or at least it seems that way to me).

○ She and her BFF are on again, off again.

○ Other girls don't come over to our house.

○ She doesn't ask to invite friends on family outings.

○ There's a lot of crying and drama over friends.

○ I've witnessed her being less than friendly to other girls (being snarky, pulling the silent treatment, rolling her eyes behind someone's back or to her face, etc.).

○ She doesn't want to go to school.

If you couldn't answer a number of those because you simply don't know, that tells you something. No dad can keep tabs on all of it, but if you're completely clueless, you might not be spending enough time around your daughter — focused time where you're not consulting your iPhone or thinking about a project at work. Not trying to put you on a guilt trip — it's just a heads up: if you don't know, try to find out.

Taking a look at what you were able to mark — or not mark — can be revealing. If more than half of the statements in List 1 were true for you and your daughter, you can rest assured that she has healthy relationships even if some of the statements in List 2 ring true. You're obviously fairly tuned in — and with some daughters (like mine) you can't help but be because they tell you more than you really want to know. Again, whatever you don't know, make it your business to check it out. She'll dig it if you do.

If you marked anything in List 2, don't rush to think there's something wrong with your child. But they *are* at least caution flags, things worth looking into. We suggest mentioning them to her mom first, since ten to one she has more information than you do on the

> **Mini-Women**
>
> *My dad seems too busy to really spend time with us without answering his phone, so I don't open up to him that much.*

subject. Watch to see if those behaviors continue. Spend some time with your daughter and broach the subject (which we'll talk about below). Pray for her. In her world, this is like you worrying about whether you're going to have a job tomorrow. It's that big a deal.

You're going to need some help.

Learning from the Master

Okay, so girls need healthy relationships with each other so they can grow into women who have healthy relationships with each other. You want your daughter to be happy and fulfilled, and this is part of that. You get it.

It's bigger than that, though. If you attend a church, you know that the women are a force to be reckoned with. As a group, they often get a ton of things done while we men are still sitting around talking about it. They can multitask, and they're aware of how what they do is going to make everybody feel, which means not only is a lot accomplished but whatever it is will be something most everybody can live with. Get a bunch of Marys and Marthas working together and look out.

We see it over and over in the Bible.

Ruth and Naomi were the team that got David's line going. Naomi got Ruth married to Boaz, and they together had Obed, who was the father of Jesse. The rest, as we say, is history.

Rachel and Leah, despite their rivalry over Jacob (started, incidentally, by their father Laban ... just saying), combined efforts and were instrumental in getting Jacob's whole tribe back to Canaan.

In the New Testament, we have the story of a group of women at Philippi who, as Luke tells it, gathered at the river to talk with Paul and his people. In that group was Lydia, who was converted, along with her entire household, and gave Paul and Silas extended hospitality. A woman of substance, Lydia had help. Female help.

Nowhere is the commitment of a group of women more vivid than in the Gospels.

[Jesus] continued according to plan, traveled to town after town, village after village, preaching God's kingdom, spreading the

*Message. The Twelve were with him. There were also some women
in their company who had been healed of various evil afflictions
and illnesses: Mary, the one called Magdalene ... Joanna ... and
Susanna ... along with many others who used their considerable
means to provide for the company.*

Luke 8:1–3, The Message

Some of these same women, along with Jesus' mother, were at the
foot of the cross at the crucifixion (John 19:25–27), a scene some of
the male disciples missed because they cut and ran when Jesus was
arrested. Matthew mentions them there too (27:55–56), as does Mark
(15:40–41). Luke shows Jesus talking directly to them, telling them
not to weep for him but for themselves and their children (23:27–31).

The loyalty of this group of women went beyond Jesus' death. All
four Gospels show the women going to the tomb together to mourn
and to care for Jesus' body. They were sent—in Matthew (28:5–7)
by an angel and in John (20:17–18) by Jesus himself—to tell the
disciples that Jesus had been resurrected from the dead. They were
the first to bear witness to the risen Lord.

Women relating to each other and working together can have
a powerful influence, particularly in the kingdom of God here on
earth. When we encourage our daughters to learn how to relate to
their female peers now, we're doing a service to the rest of society and
its future. That, as the mini-women say, is a God-thing.

Mini-
Women

*When it comes to
friend problems, my
dad is AMAZING! I
have some complaints
about him when it
comes to other issues,
but I can't complain
about this one.*

Where Do I Come In?

It's one thing to understand what's going on in the world of tween
girl politics and to get its significance. But should you actually try
to help?

Yeah, you should, just as you would if she was struggling with a
subject in school. We're talking about a social skill here. Her self-confidence, her identity, her social problem-solving ability are at stake,
which is more important than whether she can master pre-algebra.

The challenge is that you're not around when the problems arise
(unless you're shadowing her at school or listening in on all her

phone conversations). Plus, you don't have any control over how her girlfriends (or foes) behave. This is the first time in her life that she's involved in something where you can't be there. At least not while it's happening.

But you are an influence on *her* and the way she interacts with people. Since this is the area where you have the least control, you're going to want that influence to count. There are six things you can definitely do.

#1. Be aware of her friendships

You don't have to try to stay up with all the inner workings of this mysterious world, but do get a basic knowledge of who the BFFs are, their names, and how your daughter knows them. Just the fact that you know Ashley is her BFF on the soccer team and Hannah's her closest church buddy will help her see that you care. I spent a lot of time whispering to Nancy, "What's that one's name?" and until I was sure, I called them all "Sweet Pea." Once I did get them sorted out, I tried to remember something special about each one of them. I'd say, "Jessica has enough hair for thirty-seven people," which made her giggle, and Chamaea became "Mouse" because she was small and squealy. I still call her Mousie today—and she's about to give birth to her second child.

It's nice if you can get a little acquainted with your daughter's friends and let them know who you are. The more comfortable they feel in your home, the more they—and your daughter—are going to be themselves. I liked it that most of the spend-the-nights and the Saturday afternoons in the backyard playing Robin Hood took place at our house. For several reasons. One, Marijean's friends saw what our standards were so they weren't likely to try to talk her into something they knew we'd frown on. Two, I had sort of a peripheral knowledge of what they were talking about, what was big with them, and that told me a lot about my daughter. And third, we both saw how she was treating her friends and vice versa so we could hone in on any problems. There might be more of a mess in the kitchen and more noise in the family room when you're trying to watch the History Channel, but it's worth it if it means keeping yourself in the loop.

Mini-Women

I don't think my dad knows a lot of what's going on with me and my friends, but he does know enough to stay connected with me, and we can strike up a conversation about it. I usually have to fill him in on the who did what, and why so and so is mad at me and so forth.

What you don't want to do is overstep the boundaries and embarrass the kid. If she and her friends are talking about boys in the backseat on the way home from soccer practice, that's not the time to join in the conversation and tell them all to stay away from the little jackals until they're eighteen. Same goes for lecturing the whole group of BFFs on their taste in music when they're all dancing to Taylor Swift on the back deck. Poke your head in and let your daughter know you approve of the cookie baking, the scrapbooking, or the manicuring, but don't think you have to hunker down and hang out unless you're invited. Marijean asked me to make milkshakes for her and the BFF because I "made them the best," but they didn't request my presence when they were watching a movie or ask my opinion about their toenail polish.

None of that takes more than about five minutes before the gaggle of girls flits on to the next activity. But it's enough time to let you know if a friendship isn't a particularly good one for your daughter. If you see her exhibiting any of those behaviors in List 2 ("In Reality," page 117), you'll be able to see where they might be coming from. More on that below. Just know that the attention you pay to the BFFs is worth it on a number of levels.

Sometimes I wish that my dad would WANT to talk about my friends, but he never seems that interested.

#2. Teach her to not let friendships rule her

Now that we've convinced you how important girl relationships are for your tween daughter, we need to take you to the flip side of that. Especially if your daughter is a social extrovert (one dad refers to his as the "Social Coordinator"), she may spend more time making, maintaining, and managing friends than she does, oh, doing homework, getting her chores done, paying attention on the playing field, or actually focusing on the Sunday school lesson. Her teacher may tell you she could be an excellent student if she didn't talk so much in class. She may get in trouble for passing notes or coming in late from recess because she was counseling somebody out on the playground. Your only leverage with her seems to be taking away her phone, her email, her Saturday afternoon play date.

If your daughter is more of an introvert and enjoys having one or two close friends, they are probably even more important to her than a whole crowd of them is to the social butterfly. As a result, she can get into some real quandaries. Do I study for my geography test or stay on the phone and help my BFF with her problem? Do I try to sneak on the lip gloss Mom told me I can't wear because I told my girlfriends I would? Do I let my bestie copy off of my homework or risk having her mad at me for the rest of the day (which is, like, forever)?

You may not even be aware that any of that is going on, so what do you do? Several things:

Model a balance between social activities and other responsibilities. Whether you're aware of it or not, she's got you in her sights. If you blow off a family gathering to play yet another game of golf with the guys, she notices, and gets the message that friends are always more important than family (including her). If you upgrade your bike so you can compete with your buddy while her mom's car breaks down once a week, that doesn't escape your daughter. Neither does treating your wife differently (and disrespectfully) or ignoring your daughter when your friends are around. If Daddy does it, why shouldn't she?

Talk to her about priorities. Without even mentioning her BFFs, take the initiative to tell her what priorities are and help her list hers and put them in order. It won't work to tell her what they are and number them for her. Let her do it with you asking questions and making suggestions. Post them where she can see them. Next time an issue comes up—"I can't clean my room! Madison invited me to go the mall with her and her mom!"—you can refer her to the list she made herself.

Praise her when she makes a good choice. Too often we don't say anything at all until they mess up, and then we're all over them like white on rice. A little positive reinforcement goes a lot further than jumping on every mistake she makes. She is, after all, a kid and she's going to make a lot of them. The well-placed "Nice job on those grades this time, Kiddo. I know you didn't get to spend as much time with your friends, but I'm proud of you"—that's what we're talking about.

Don't make HER friendships YOUR last priority. If she knows you'll set aside time to take her and the BFFs to a movie or stay home so she can have them over while her mom's out, she probably won't whine

Mini-Women

My dad is pretty great when it comes to my friends. He's good at getting them to crack up. I have lots of social stuff and he's good about helping me with people who (we're being honest here) bug the socks off of me! Now that I think about it, my friends and even not-so-friends are really one of his high points in my opinion.

when you don't have room in your schedule at any given moment. We're not saying be available to play chauffeur 24/7. In fact, planning ahead, putting it on your schedule to drive to softball practice every Thursday or take everybody to the opening of the next Pixar movie shows her how to plan her own social life around her responsibilities. You really do gain a lot more ground by example than you ever can in a twenty-minute lecture (most of which she isn't going to hear anyway).

#3. Help her work out friendship problems if she comes to you

We covered "how to help without doing it for her" pretty thoroughly in chapter 1, but it bears repeating here. When she honors you by coming to you with an issue she's having with another girl (besides bullying, which we'll go into below), steer away from trying to fix it by telling her what she should do. This is the perfect opportunity to show her how to think things through and look at her options before coming up with a plan. If she decides she's going to approach it in some way you know isn't going to end well, you can warn her, but if she insists on doing it her way, let her go for it. When things turn south, the consequences won't be life-ending (though she'll think so at the time), and she'll have learned a valuable lesson. If she makes a good decision and the problem is solved, her confidence soars because she figured it out herself. That isn't going to happen if she just does what you tell her to do with said friend. And if you give her direction and it messes up the whole friendship, guess who gets the blame.

#4. Talk to her about cliques

She knows what they are, though she may be pleasantly surprised that *you* know what they are. This discussion is more about whether there are cliques at school or church or in the home school co-op. Whether her group of friends is a clique. What her feelings are about being in one—does she want to be, does she see that they're not healthy? You're mostly just asking questions and letting her tell you what she knows. If her thinking is skewed, you have the perfect opportunity to say, "Really? 'Cause, see, I don't get why anybody would want to be friends with those girls when they treat people like dirt. Is there something I'm not seeing?" If you can keep judgment of her and an "I'm going to straighten you out" attitude out of it, you can learn and teach a lot that may save your daughter—and you—some real heartache.

#5. Help her deal with bullying

This one isn't optional. It applies even if she says she doesn't want your help or denies that it's happening even though you have evidence that it is. You can't take intimidation and aggression against your daughter lightly.

We're not about going in there and taking care of it *for* her. We're saying the minute you know what's going on, let her know you're on her side. Then be there, in the following ways:

Do not tell her that if she would do this, this, and this, she wouldn't be a target. That makes it sound like you think it's her fault, and it isn't. Yes, girls who are timid and lacking in self-confidence are more vulnerable to bullying, but the treatment your shy, awkward daughter receives still says nothing about who she is and everything about who the bully is. Just to refresh your memory, in the words of blogger Mary Dixon LeBeau, "These [bullies] are girls who bond over their mutual disdain for those who don't quite match their ilk."[10] Makes your lip curl, doesn't it? So avoid uttering any of the following, or your daughter won't believe for a minute that you're her ally:

Don't Say It, Dude …

"Why do you put up with that?"

"Don't let people do that to you."

"Don't be a wimp—stand up to them."

"Give her some of what she's giving you."

"If you don't do something about it, I will."

"I got bullied too when I was your age. It makes you tougher."

"I think you're too sensitive. You let it get to you too much."

"You're giving them what they want. Just ignore them and they'll leave you alone."

"If you wouldn't walk around like you're afraid of everybody, these kids wouldn't pick on you."

Picture yourself at gunpoint—several gunpoints—with nowhere to turn and nobody there to help. Your life is on the line. When you somehow escape, and the bad guys get away, imagine somebody telling you, "Why did you put up with that? Why did you let them do that to you? You were a wimp—you should've stood up to them. You let them get to you. You should have just ignored them."

That's what it feels like to your tween daughter when she comes crying to you that the "guns" are being pointed at her and nobody's doing anything about it—and you tell her she's responsible for making it stop and that she did something wrong that made it start in the first place.

Besides, none of those statements is true. She's not putting up with it; she's trying not to make it worse. She's not a wimp; she's rightfully scared. If she tries to bully back, she'll only exacerbate the situation, especially since she can't hold her own, nor do you want her to. Do you really want her to be "tough"? I personally didn't want my daughter to be so hard-core she was unmoved when somebody attacked her very being. She's not a Marine, for Pete's sake. Ignoring doesn't work—we'll show you what does. But you'll never get as far as sharing any of that with her if you suggest to her that this whole thing is her fault. It's nobody's fault but the bully's. Make sure she understands that.

Let her know she isn't in this alone. Before you even ask for details, make sure she understands that you are there for her and you'll find a way to keep her safe. Get her mother involved. Give her the security of a family who has her back. She's going to have to fight this battle on her own (except in extreme cases), but she can't do it without the support of the people she trusts the most.

Get the whole story. If she believes that you're going to walk with her through this no matter how small or how intense the bullying is, she won't exaggerate or understate. Keep asking questions until she's out of information. Then you can determine whether she's in physical danger—in which case all bets are off and you're headed for the school or the parents of the bully if the abuse is taking place anywhere other than the school grounds. If the abuse is verbal, and therefore emotional and mental, and it's affecting her schoolwork, her health, or her emotional stability, you'll want to alert her teachers, coaches, whatever adults need to be involved, just to let them know that you're aware of the situation and that you're guiding your daughter through it. They may give you additional information based on their observations.

Just don't let them tell you your daughter is overreacting or being dramatic to get attention. Most kids don't tattle on bullies, much less make more out of the situation than it is. They're ashamed and afraid; they're not going to go through this for something that isn't real. Stand up for your daughter.

Other adults may also give you: "So-and-So is bullying her? I find that hard to believe. She's such a sweet girl." Part of a Mean Girl's success is her chameleon ability to change to suit the situation. Teachers are often flabbergasted when they find out their pretty, smart, cooperative pet is wreaking havoc on half the girls in the fourth grade. RMGs make it a point to ingratiate themselves with the right people. Kind of scary, isn't it?

Give her some concrete direction. If the bullying hasn't escalated to a dangerous level, the best thing you can do for your daughter is arm her with practical methods. Start by forgetting just about everything you've always believed about dealing with bullies, especially boy bullies. This is what she needs to know:

The goal is not to change the bully or make her a friend. The goal is for your daughter to take back the power to be herself no matter what anybody's saying.

Ignoring only works if you do it right away, the first time. If she's ever reacted to this bully, she can forget trying to act like she's invisible.

If she wants to try ignoring, she needs to look bored or annoyed, not scared or hurt. This is one time it's okay to pretend she doesn't feel the way she really does. It's normal to *be* upset, but she can't show the bully that she is.

Any verbal response she does make shouldn't be with the same attitude the bully is using. Not tit for tat, eye for eye. She needs to stay as calm as possible, look the bully in the eye, and say something like:

"Okay, well, if that's the way you want to be, that's your problem."

"You know what, I really don't need this."

"Are you having a bad day?"

"That's weird. I don't remember asking for your opinion."

"Come on, you're better than this." (Nancy always asks the mini-women she does bullying workshops with, "What's she going to say, 'No, I am not better than this'?")

As soon as the words are out of her mouth, she needs to turn and walk away. That's what "turn the other cheek" means in a situation like this.

If the bully keeps her from going to her locker or getting to her class on time, she should ask some other girls to walk with her. This is not to form a bully gang of her own or create any kind of intimidation. (We're not talking *Revenge of the Nerds* here.) A bully won't try to block the way of five or six people. The girls she asks don't have to take the bully on. They're just part of safety in numbers.

If she feels physically threatened or has been injured, she needs to go to the nearest adult and tell. This isn't kindergarten playground tattling. This is serious informing. If she's not believed, she needs to keep telling adults until she finds someone who will help her. If there is no one, she's to call you or her mom.

With all of those steps in mind, help your daughter form a plan that fits her situation. Role play with her if that works for the two of you. Tell her she can do this, because she can.

Don't allow her to go on feeling powerless. Point out opportunities for her to make other friends; don't just tell her to go do it. Show her that she's a special human being by giving her attention, asking her opinion, talking about the good she does. Make sure she knows that other people's opinions of her are just that—opinions. They don't mean that's who she is. Open up possibilities for her to shine. Maybe it's time for some classes for that budding artistic talent. Could be she's ready to audition for a play or take tennis lessons—things she enjoys that don't involve girls who are salivating for a chance to belittle her. She'll be able to reaffirm her self-worth, and chances are she won't be bullied again.

Teach her to expect to be respected and not to tolerate any forms of disrespect. Start, of course, by always treating *her* with respect.

Let her school know that you won't tolerate bullying in your child's place of learning. Know the school's policy on bullying and make sure it's enforced. Talk to other parents, the teachers, and the coaches and let them know how you feel about kids being afraid in the environment they are required to spend most of their day in. Moms should do this too, but your male presence is essential. Be perfectly okay with bringing the full power of your testosterone to bear when it comes to protecting your daughter—short of punching out the principal, of course.

Approach cyberbullying differently. If your daughter is the victim of cyberbullying, walk through the steps together. She shouldn't reply to any kind of communication that's abusive or obscene. The first time it happens, she should ignore it and hang up or log off. If it happens again, even once, you contact the service provider (Yahoo, Hotmail, Verizon, AT&T, etc.) and ask for a number to call to report abusive messaging. Call it. You can even forward nasty emails to your service provider. If the abuse continues, save all the evidence—print out emails, save text messages, don't delete voice mail. You'll need it to take action. Try to find out who's doing the bullying. In Outlook or Outlook Express, for example, you can right click over an email to reveal details about where and who the email came from. That puts you in a position to contact a parent or the service provider. If a bullying message was sent from a school computer, contact the school administration immediately. Keep reminding your tween that this is telling, not tattling. If cyberbullying is happening on a website, find out who hosts the site and report it. If physical threats are made on line or by phone, call the police. I'm serious. *Cyberbullying is against the law. Don't put up with it.*

If your daughter isn't a victim, chances are she's seen bullying go on. Make her aware of what you now know about it and get her to talk to you about what she's witnessed. Discuss what she and her friends can do to put a stop to it. A whole chapter of Nancy's book *Girl Politics: Friends, Cliques, and Really Mean Chicks* is devoted to anti-bullying. You might want to pick up a copy for your daughter.

#6. Hold your daughter responsible if she's a Mean Girl

Before you skip this section because your Princess would never do any of this stuff you've just been shaking your head over, hear us out. A tween girl bully is not rotten to the core. There are always reasons for the things kids do, and they are sometimes painful. Wouldn't you want to know that your daughter is suffering from something that makes her behave like Cruella de Vil so you can help her?

How do you know if she's behaving like a bully? You'll see these signs:

Put-down language when she talks about other girls (loser, lame, stupid, butt-ugly).

Endless arguing and sulking when she's with friends.

Trouble following rules.

No trouble manipulating her way out of following said rules.

Calls from mothers saying your daughter is mean to hers.

No remorse if she's confronted on that; that other girl is obviously a crybaby.

Routinely blowing up over small issues.

Instant frustration when things don't go her way.

Even if she isn't bullying, those behaviors warrant some looking into. There are any number of reasons why she would act like that.

Some stem from the world she lives in. She sees sniping and clever put-downs rewarded. She watches "mean" TV and listens to snarky DJs on the radio. She buys into the "girl power" philosophy.

Some are responding to what's going on at home. If she's yelled at and belittled, that's how she's learned to treat people. If the only way to get attention is to grab it, that's what she does. If she's been allowed to run the household with her demands, why shouldn't she run the fifth grade?

Some are even influenced by, dare we say it, the church. Idealistic tweens can take the concept of being "unsaved" to extremes and become little Pharisees, looking down on girls who don't know Christ and excluding them, informing them they're going to hell and spreading rumors that they're atheists or Satan worshipers.

In almost every case, there's either jealousy and insecurity involved or an over-the-top sense of entitlement. You aren't doing her any favors by letting it go on. She may have "power" and be "popular," but she isn't well liked and she isn't developing relationship skills. Just as you wouldn't tolerate aggression *against* your daughter, you really can't tolerate aggression *by* her.

So what do you do?

Confront her behavior. If you were ever going to curb your urge to blow a gasket, this would be the time. She needs a calm, direct, non-judgmental approach. "I know you're not an awful person, but you have to stop treating people this way. We're going to find out what's going on with you so you can be the real you." Stay with it until she admits she's been wrong. Don't go into reasons. Don't roll out the consequences. Just get her to take responsibility.

Make sure she gets it that she has no right to insult, intimidate, threaten, or abuse another human being, no matter what her "reasons" are. If you know she's coming by her ugliness honestly, as in, from her home life, promise her that you're going to change that even if it means changing yourself.

Once she owns up, give her credit for that. She can't think of herself as bad at the core if she's going to change. Tell her she can turn the natural power she seems to have into something good.

Encourage her to go to God and lay it all out. Offer to pray with her or give her the space and time to do it on her own. Make sure she knows she has to have God's help if she's going to turn this around.

Then help her figure out why she ever thought bullying was a good idea. If you can't get to the bottom of it together, seek professional help. There's no more shame in that than there is in getting her to an orthopedic surgeon if she has a broken leg.

When you're convinced she wants to change, suggest these steps for her to take. This doesn't constitute punishment, so don't make her do them in order to get un-grounded. (We don't even encourage you to ground her in the first place.) She can go to the girls she's hurt and ask their forgiveness without expecting that to make everything okay. She can tell her fellow bulliers she isn't going to be the mean girl anymore even if it means losing them as friends; now that she's nicer, she'll have different and better ones. She can get rid of or avoid anything that trips her meanness trigger and fill that space with things that bring out the best in her. If she was a "Christian bully," she can apologize to the people she spiritually mugged and offer to talk to them about how cool it is to be a Christ follower.

———————

Through all of this—the normal ups and downs of girl relationships, the friend funkiness that needs to be learned through, and the downright ugliness of bullying—the most important thing you can do is model how to treat people and how to respond if they treat her badly. Even if you forget everything you've just read or you talk till you have laryngitis and it still doesn't seem to be sinking in, don't ever stop showing your daughter how a person of integrity behaves. If you respect the dignity of every human being, including her, she has a strong chance of doing the same.

Bridging the Gap

Father, I may never comprehend just what goes on when they're giggling and squabbling and running to the bathroom en masse. I just know whatever it is, it's important to my daughter. Please bridge the gap between what she needs to learn about relationships and what I have in me to teach her. Can't do it without you. Counting on you, Father.

Amen.

7

I Liked It Better When Boys Had Cooties

What Just Happened?

You're settled in together for some daddy-daughter time. She has the popcorn—you have the remote for the DVD player. Life is good. Especially since you were able to find a PG movie that doesn't require as much Parental Guidance as a walk down Bourbon Street.

Or so you thought when you reviewed it ahead of time.

But you're not five minutes into the film when your tween daughter points to the teenage boy on the screen and says, "Now, *he's* hot."

You press PAUSE.

"You have to go to the bathroom already?" she says.

"He's 'hot'?" you say.

"Oh, yeah."

Your mind races through all the possible responses. *You're too young to think some guy is "hot." How did you come up with that anyway? Who have you been talking to? That's it—I'm putting you in lockdown until you're eighteen. No—make that twenty-one.*

"Da-ad," she says. "Can we watch the movie?"

"Just a second," you say. This is obviously a turning point in your relationship with your daughter, and you don't want to mess it up. You feel like you already have, or she wouldn't be making statements like that, right?

"Dad? Hello?"

Mini-Women

My dad and I don't talk about boys. I guess it'd be okay if we did, but maybe a little awkward. It's like that for a lot of girls.

You turn to her and try to modulate your voice to something Cliff Huxtable would approve of.

"What exactly does *hot* mean?" you ask.

Her eyes widen. "You don't know?"

"I know." All too well. "I just want to see if you think it means what I think you think it means."

"Huh?" she says.

Yeah. You're blowing it.

"Okay—what do you mean when you say that guy's 'hot'?"

She shrugs. "It just means he's cute."

You stare. "That's it?"

"Well, ye-ah." Her gaze shifts longingly to the remote.

"What's cute about him?" you say.

"I don't know. He's just not lame like the boys I know."

Your heart lifts. "So . . . you don't personally know any boys your age who are hot."

"No!" she says, almost overturning the popcorn bag. "Gross. All the boys I know are absurd little creeps. Can we just watch the movie now?"

You nod and press PLAY. Yet your mind is still whirling. It's a relief to know that she's not associating daily with anybody she considers "hot." But the fact that there's something about that stud on the screen that she knows is desirable, even if she can't tell you what it is . . . that may be the scariest thought you've ever had.

You make a note to self: look for an all-girl school.

————

We saved this topic for last for two reasons. One, if we'd started with it, you might have broken into a sweat and chucked the book altogether. Not many fathers of tween daughters are ready for this right out of the chute.

The second reason is that everything we've talked about so far—your daughter's image of her physical self, the changes taking place in her body, her understanding of who she is and her ability to be that, and the development of relationship skills through other girls—comes together when she realizes that boys might not be so bad after all.

You may have been dreading this ever since potty training was out of the way because what else is there to dread in raising a girl? Or maybe you decided when she was born that this was one thing you didn't have to worry about because you were going to keep her away from all things male until she was twenty-five, and then you were going to choose a husband for her (after doing a thorough background check and conducting an in-depth interrogation). Or maybe you're like one dad we know who, the first time he held his adopted baby daughter in his arms, looked at the tiny fourth finger on her left hand and burst into tears because he knew someday some other guy was going to put a ring on it and take her away from him.

If your daughter is a tween, the time has come to at least start thinking about the inevitable place of boys in her life. And if you think you feel out of the loop when it comes to her relationships with *girls*, you haven't seen anything yet—unless you find out now what's healthy and what's not at this age, where your daughter is on it and where she's headed, and what you can do to help her make good choices when it comes to guys.

And no, you won't be making them for her. But your influence on her in terms of the boys and men she has relationships with in the future and what those relationships will be like is huge. Nancy started telling me this when Marijean was five years old: you are the one who shapes her attitude toward men, the one who shows her how she should expect to be treated by them, the one who models for her what a man's love is.

We'd say "no pressure," but it's on. It's a good thing, though. Whatever your daughter sees in you and hears from you, she's going to believe. Get the essentials right, and you'll give her the best chance she has for real happiness in her relationships with men.

Mini-
Women

My dad talks to me about boys. He says he'll kick the butt of the first guy who asks me out.

Here's the Deal

A number of things are normal and healthy about the boy thing at this age, and knowing what they are will relieve your mind. There are also things you need to be aware of that, as in all the other areas we've touched on, may push your daughter too far ahead of herself.

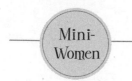

I don't have boys who are friends. Boys are "ick" to me.

My dad just doesn't seem to understand that I'm not a little girl anymore. Whenever I mention hanging out with boys AS FRIENDS, he gets all tense and has this worried kind of look. He just doesn't get that it's okay to have boys as friends at the age of twelve. I wish he could understand that. But I'm sure all dads are that way.

To help you know what you can relax about and enjoy (okay, maybe *enjoy* is too strong a word . . .) and what you need to watch over carefully, there are five things we think you need to know about boys and your tween daughter.

Why a Tween Girl Hates Boys

She doesn't actually hate them. She just uses that word because hyperbole is the default tween girl means of expression. She definitely gets annoyed with them, though. Nobody else can make her lose control and spit, scream, or spew verbal venom like a tween boy, unless it's her little brother. What's that about, anyway? She puts up with all manner of mildly despicable behavior from her best friend, but a boy even looks like he's going to say something rude and she practically goes off the deep end.

Part of that is because boys do things on purpose just to make girls lose it. It's in their contract. It's why Nancy and her Mini-Women refer to them as ALCs (Absurd Little Creeps). Do you remember why *you* did it as a kid? Partly because it was fun, but it does go deeper than that, and it's the rare tween boy who's actually aware of what compels him to mock how a girl laughs or do the armpit fart in front of her in the lunch line. He wants female attention, but he doesn't know what to do with real interaction at this point, so he resorts to whatever will make her aware of his existence but won't require him to engage in actual conversation with her. Part of his inability to show any social skills with girls whatsoever comes from the fact that girls typically mature faster than boys, and the difference is obvious in the tween years. The chance that a girl might want him to look into her eyes or talk about his feelings is terrifying. Better to treat her to a nice burp and let it go at that.

It's that same higher level of social maturity that makes girls look upon boys their own age with disdain. They really do find all that focus on bodily functions disgusting, and they're embarrassed by the teasing boys are so good at in their tweens. When a tween boy is around girls, especially the ones he secretly finds attractive, nothing seems to go through his brain before it comes out of his mouth. Out comes a snarky comment about a girl's wild, frizzy red hair when what he's really drawn to are her blue eyes. We're generalizing here. There are some really nice boys out there whose parents have taught them how to treat people. But girls tend to lump them together, declare that they have cooties, one and all, and continue to cry foul every time they come near.

Most dads are pretty okay with that.

Why a Tween Girl Likes Boys

Yes, she likes them at the same time that she holds them in contempt. The balance actually shifts as the tween years progress, from "I hate all boys!" to "Okay, some boys are all right" to "When did so many boys get to be cute?"

Mini-Women

I feel like boys haven't gotten any less obnoxious. I just don't mind as much.

It is not a sign that your tween daughter has become boy crazy and you need to think about a convent for her if she comments that a certain boy is cute (or "hot," which to her is the same thing). It's a good sign if she has boys who are friends; as she gets older she discovers that they gossip less than girls and definitely don't get into the same drama that girls do. She might even have a crush, which we'll break down for you shortly.

All of that is physically and psychologically normal. Her hormones attract her to the opposite sex. Otherwise, the human race would come to a screeching halt. Developmentally, she's right where she's supposed to be. Things are moving according to Divine Plan. You're the one who decided she needs to be a little girl forever.

At the same time that all that is going on within her, the occasional same-age boy rises to the surface with some decent manners, the ability to carry on a conversation that doesn't include insults, and a way of walking that makes her little heart do something weird. That's because the boys, if you'll recall, are going through their own hormonal changes and preadolescent development. A few of them are discovering that if they're actually nice to girls, they get better results. Both are turning into civilized human beings who will someday look for mates. It's a long process that starts with the first tiny heart flutters.

Why She Falls in Love with Teen Idols

Not that many boys are interested in "romance" at ten, and, truth be told, girls may dream of it, but they're just as frightened of it as boys. It's much safer to have a crush on a celebrity she has no hope of meeting. She can admire him from afar, put his posters up on her wall, and daydream about going on a date with him, all without the risk of not being loved back. It's great practice in dealing with feelings, because these can't hurt her.

While a younger tween is prone to attachments to members of boy bands and actors on the Disney Channel, a girl of eleven or twelve may turn her secret affections to an adult male she knows—that young math teacher, her youth pastor, the college guy who helps coach her soccer team. She may imagine herself having long, deep conversations with him, but the minute he actually looks her way, she stammers like Porky Pig because she really wants it to be one-sided. She can have enough innocent attention from him to make her pulse race but never have to worry about what to do next. Meanwhile, she's forming her vision of what she wants in a man, and her crushes are giving her valuable input.

Mini-Women

Me + Justin Bieber =
♥ ♥ ♥

What "Going Out" Means at This Age

When girls this young talk about "going out" with boys, I always want to ask, where are they going? And who's taking them? Don't these girls have fathers? The first time a boy showed up at our house to hang out with Marijean when she was in sixth grade, I said to Nancy, "That little son of a gun better stand clear." I mean, come on. Dating? At eleven?

You can relax, Dad, because when tweens say they're "going out," they're just referring to all "boyfriend-girlfriend" stuff. That's not very reassuring until you look at what having a boyfriend means to a tween girl. From what the mini-women have divulged, it looks something like this:

You like one boy better than the rest, for today at least, and you find out he likes you too this week. So you maybe write each other

As a tween, it's not actually "going out." It's mostly sitting together at lunch and at recess, but sometimes you might go walk around together — if you're both allowed.

My BFF says "going out" is hanging out with a guy at his house. I thought that was called a play date.

Going out doesn't mean anything at my age. You don't even do anything. I think people do it just for the drama. I don't want a boyfriend at twelve years old, but I do wonder why my friend has one. I think she was pressured into it.

notes, or look at each other across the classroom, or walk to the cafeteria together, only you probably don't eat lunch together because his friends would tease him and then he'd have to break up with you. There might be a phone call or two, and things may get more interesting if some other girl likes your boyfriend, especially if it's your BFF, in which case *you* would have to break up with *him*, because BFFs always trump boyfriends. You might cry when you break up, but probably not, and not like you would if you and your BFF stopped being friends.

Why It Still Seems Too Soon

It really is all pretty innocent and harmless. But still, you have to wonder, isn't it happening earlier than in past generations? Actually not. Nancy says she remembers romances blossoming in the second half of sixth grade, and that was fifty years ago. Elementary school teachers tell us that's still the mysteriously consistent time when boys and girls start simultaneously noticing each other and blushing.

Mini-Women

Some of my friends are already "going out" with their crushes in fourth grade. But it never seems to turn out, so I stay out of it. I just like being a kid.

What's changed, according to school psychologist Bryan Greeson, is the amount of freedom tweens have to act on their crushes.[1] There's more together time in coed activities. More kids have their own cell phones. Some parents even facilitate early dating by driving preteen couples to the movies and dropping them off. Like I said, don't these girls have fathers?

The whole KGOY (Kids Getting Older Younger) attitude being pushed by everybody from toy makers to clothing lines is partly responsible for that. They give both tweens and their parents the impression that this generation is somehow more sophisticated than the one before it, and that girls and boys are ready for things their older sisters and brothers weren't at their age. The logic in that eludes me, but it has some moms and dads already giving up their influence on their daughters' future dating activities and even encouraging them to go with the trend. Throw in all the suggestive sexual stuff they're exposed to in the media and it's no wonder ten-year-old girls are thinking they need to get themselves a boyfriend and be "sexy," whatever that is.

That's what dads need to worry about. Not whether their tween daughter has a crush on Zac Efron or giggles with her friends over who in the sixth grade is "cute" (or "hot" …), but whether she is being pushed into stuff nobody's ready for at ten or eleven—or even sixteen. It's not what's happening inside of her that you need to fight, but the world around her that's trying to steal her innocence.

In Reality

Before you take up your role as the main influencer in your daughter's romantic future—or continue it if you already figured out that's what you are—it's good to have some idea where she is on the scale from "Boys gross me out and make me feel icky!" to "I have a BF." (Note the lack of the additional F. Even she realizes this is not forever.)

You know the drill. Mark the statements that are true for your daughter … at least, as far as you can tell.

My daughter:

1. never talks about boys in any context; they might as well not exist as far as she's concerned.

Mini-Women

I had a lot of boys that were friends when I was younger. One time one of my guy friends and I wanted to have a sleepover. I couldn't understand why that wasn't okay, so my dad explained it to me. I still didn't understand because, after all, I was only eight.

2. makes it clear in no uncertain terms that all boys are absurd little creeps (ALCs).

3. mentions some ALCs but doesn't think the whole gender is hopeless and disgusting.

4. has a crush on a celebrity (as in posters plastered on her bedroom walls, his music on repeat on the CD player, squeals when he appears on TV).

5. seems to admire an adult male figure in her life (besides you, of course).

6. seems to get along with boys as well as she does with girls.

7. seems to get along better with her boy friends than she does with the girls in her life.

8. has a close boy friend (not to be confused with a BF—she can talk to this person without blushing).

9. gets teased about her close boyfriend and blows it off.

10. gets teased about her close boyfriend and loudly proclaims that he is NOT her BF.

11. has mentioned a boy's name in a way that you know he's BF material.

If I like a boy, I keep it to myself or I get teased by my dad for a long time. I don't mind that much, but the hard part is keeping a straight face while I tell him it's not true.

Mini-Women

I want to marry a Christian man, one much like my dad. There are some things I like about my dad that have made me say, "I want that in my husband" — like the way he always tells my mom she's beautiful. But there are some things where I go, "Whoa, I need to make sure that I do NOT marry someone like that. Like, someone un-Christian ..."

When my dad talks to me about boys, he doesn't give me any advice. Mostly he sits and listens to me talk. And teases me, which I like. I want the man I marry to have some of the same characteristics as my dad, like being able to make me laugh, and listening to how I feel.

12. turns red and protests when you tease her about a possible BF.
13. has asked you if it's okay if she has a BF at school.
14. has announced that she and some boy are "going out."
15. talks nonstop about boys—all boys—all the time.
16. has asked you to drive her and a boy someplace for a "date."
17. likes to hang out with boys older than she is and dresses for the occasion.

You'll want to look at the particular statements you checked off so you'll know what applies as we move on. In general, though, if you marked anything from 1 through 12, those are things you should be able to live with. She's normal and healthy, so why would you want to change any of that?

If you realized any of the statements from 13 to 17 are true, that doesn't mean your daughter's already got a love life you know nothing about. But the further up you go, the more attention you need to pay and the sooner you're going to want to lay some ground rules with her. We'll cover all of that in the "Where Do I Come In?" section. Let's turn first to what the ultimate Parent has to say about it.

Mini-Women

When I was a tween, I wasn't interested in boys. But my dad did sometimes talk about, casually, someday meeting "the one" and how guys would someday be "interesting" to me. Of course, at that age, I cringed at the thought of having a crush on a boy. I thought the girls who cooed over boys were off their rockers.

Learning from the Master

When the human race began to increase, with more and more daughters being born, the sons of God noticed that the daughters of men were beautiful.

Genesis 6:1, *The Message*

It's been happening since the beginning. The daughters of men start becoming beautiful, and the sons start noticing. It's as natural as birds building nests and bees—well, you get the idea. Rachel noticed Jacob when she was still virtually a kid by today's standards (albeit one with a great figure, evidently). Esther was made queen as a still-blossoming teenager. Mary was chosen to be the mother of Christ when, by most scholarly estimates, she was probably about fourteen.

God set it up that girls would become attractive to boys and boys would respond. We can't argue with that. And yet as dads, we often do.

We think, *She shouldn't even be thinking about boys. She's too young to even know what love is. If I let her have a boyfriend when she's twelve, she'll be pregnant by the time she's sixteen.*

When we get into that, we're not only denying the attraction that's hormonally and psychologically there but we're also missing the other part of what's shown to us by God in these matters, and that's the role of the fathers.

We can't depend too much on the Old Testament dads. Laban used his daughters to play Jacob (Genesis 29), and when Jacob's daughter Dinah was raped, he was ticked off at his sons for avenging the travesty and putting *his* name in jeopardy (Genesis 34). Saul treated his daughter Michal like a pawn in a political game. And David, though furious that his son Amnon had raped and then discarded his sister Tamar, isn't reported to have done a thing about it. Tamar "lived in her brother Absalom's house, a desolate woman" (2 Samuel 13:20).

Those fathers were somewhat bound by the customs and political climate of their day. You are not. Jesus took care of that. Your only obligation is to follow his precise instructions:

> *"Don't push these children away. Don't ever get between them and me. These children are at the very center of life in the kingdom."*
>
> Mark 10:14, *The Message*

He doesn't say, "Deny your children their feelings and their delights." He says love them, as you do him.

So we don't tell our daughters they shouldn't be giving boys a second thought, any more than we tell them not to have a period or grow breasts. What we do is teach them about love and purity and honesty and self-respect. We welcome their questions and take them in our arms when they feel pushed around, and we model living a life that honors God.

You'll still worry the first time she goes out on a date with a boy, sometime in the future. Way in the future. When that time comes, you'll still want to examine prospective boyfriends under a bare lightbulb. But don't deny her the right to feel how she feels. Just show her how to examine those feelings and live them out in a godly way.

Does my dad talk to me about boys? Ha! He leaves that up to Mom.

When my dad talked to me about boys, he wasn't all demanding or telling me what to think or do, but shared HIS opinion and told me that if I had any different thoughts, we could talk about it. Which I thought was totally cool. All dads should talk to their girls like that.

Your first help comes from God, so start praying—like you haven't been doing that already. We'll back that up with a few suggestions.

Where Do I Come In?

My dad didn't, like, give me "the talk" or anything like that. For most of my tween years, I was too embarrassed to talk with him about it even though I had a LOT of questions and confusing thoughts.

Wherever your daughter is on the boy-thing scale and whatever your thinking is in terms of her future dating life, there are five things that pretty much all dads of tween daughters need to do—or at least consider.

Help her see how feminine she is. At the same time she's starting to want boys to think she's pretty, they step up the teasing because they're afraid of how pretty she's becoming. Her image of herself as a lovely feminine girl can go down the tubes after five minutes in geography class. She needs your reassurance that she's a delightful almost-woman, and she'll believe you far more readily than she will her mother. You, after all, were a boy once, and you know what they like.

How to do that? Girls on Nancy's tween blog overwhelmingly voted for the Daddy Date, which we've mentioned before. Not only is it a fun way to get to know your daughter better, but it gives you a chance to show her what *you* know about her that she might not know about herself. Try dinner at someplace a little higher on the food chain than McDonald's. A surprise trip to the mall for a new outfit. A card just from you on Valentine's Day. That all proves to her that she's a female worth loving.

Her mom shows her how to act like a girl. You show her what it feels like to be one.

Listen to where she is with boys. This is especially important if you weren't able to mark off much on the "In Reality" list, pages 141–142, but it also applies to those who think they have their daughters pegged. Girls' ideas are changing rapidly at this age. You'd be surprised what you'll find out if you'll (a) ask and (b) actually hear her out without laying down a bunch of rules for how it's going to be. We'll get to that. This talk is as much about your relationship with her as it is about the subject of boys. You're establishing a connection so she feels comfortable coming to you.

What to ask? It isn't rocket science. When the two of you are alone—definitely when there are no brothers present—and you are undistracted, just ask her what she thinks about boys. Are they still absurd little creeps? Are some of them nice? Do girls in her class have boyfriends? What does "going out" mean to her? Don't grill her, obviously. You probably won't have to. If they know you're not waiting to pounce on them, most tween girls will give you a good twenty minutes on any one of those questions.

Do you *just* listen? At first. Once she winds down, and depending on what she's expressed to you, you can give her your basic thoughts and even begin to work together to establish some guidelines. At this age, those might include:

- Keeping boy-stuff in perspective, as in, it's not the biggest deal in life.
- Dealing with any peer pressure to have a boyfriend when she couldn't care less.
- Getting to know boys as friends rather than emphasizing the romance thing.
- Prepping her for how to respond to dares and teasing.
- Discussing what age is appropriate for real dating.

Mini-Women

My dad says things like "I don't think girls should ask boys out, but the other way around," and "There are boundaries in every relationship," and "You shouldn't be afraid to dump a boy if you have to." Except that he doesn't say that word for word. He says it in that daddy kinda way. You know. Long.

Mini-Women

My dad's strict attitude about boys makes me feel like I can't even be friends with boys, which makes me annoyed and confused and feel bad about myself, because everybody else seems fine talking with them.

Every time my dad sees a motorcycle, he tells me that I'm not allowed to date a guy who even owns a motorcycle. Once he said that when ALL my brother's friends were in the car. It was embarrassing for everyone except my dad, and I felt like crying.

Setting major taboos on music that puts sex and violence together or encourages promiscuity, as well as anything rated R (and actually *using* parental guidance on PG-13 movies).

The three things you don't want to do when you're chatting about boys:

Pry for information (best way going to get her to clam up).

Tease her in a way she clearly doesn't like (which is usually because *you* are uncomfortable).

Launch into a lecture instead of teaching her how to make good choices—because in the privacy of her inner life, she'll be the one making them, not you.

Mini- Women

When I was a tween, I preferred my guy friends over my girl- friends. I think my dad kind of enjoyed it, me being his little tomboy who managed to hold her own with all the boys.

Should you talk to her about sex? Only if she asks, and only after you and her mother have discussed how you're going to approach it. We agreed that we would answer any question Marijean asked and give her only as much information as she needed at that moment. I have to admit it was a relief that she didn't come to me with any until she was a teenager. Tween girls are usually confused and embarrassed enough about the mysterious workings of their changing bodies and how that connects with sex without discussing all that with their dads. Just be ready in case it comes up, as it did for one dad we know. While his wife was out of town, their nine-year-old asked to know where babies came from. He said he felt totally out of his element without a PowerPoint program.

Give her the male perspective. It's a really bad idea to put all dealings with boys on your daughter's mother, even if you don't live together. What kind of sense does that make, really? *You* are the one who knows how a boy's mind works. *You* are the one who can see how mini-men are going to view her. Why would you make this whole thing her mom's responsibility when she doesn't know as much about it as you do?

You are your daughter's only chance right now for seeing things from a boy's point of view, and she needs that if boys are going to become people to her rather than remain mysterious creatures she may either run from or be so enchanted by she can't think about anything else.

And we're talking here about an honest perspective—not what you want her to think about boys so she'll stay away from them. For example, is it really your experience that all boys "only want one thing"? Can you tell her instead that it's possible to be friends with a boy? Can you teach her how to spot a nice guy as well as how to develop a jerk radar? Can you explain to her what boys are going through so she'll have some compassion for them—rather than scream every time they knock her pencil off her desk to get her attention?

If you do that, you're establishing an open communication between the two of you, so that as she gets older and does have relationships with boys, she'll continue to ask for your insights and share some of what's going on—although you're never going to hear it all. She's going to believe that she can have an emotional and even a spiritual relationship with a good guy without having sex. She'll be convinced that not everybody is "doing it." She'll know all that because of you and the foundation you're laying now, when you're just talking about liking boys rather than about how to resist having anything to do with them.

Show respect for her healthy relationships with boys. We know one dad who threatened to wear his DADD T-shirt every time a boy came around his twelve-year-old daughter. (For the uninitiated, that's Dads Against Daughters Dating.) He was kidding. A lot of dads aren't. It's like they think it's their duty to make this whole thing as uncomfortable for their daughters as possible. Either that, or they don't see the effect they're having. Hard to miss the tears and the, you guessed it, running off to the bathroom. That won't happen for long. Even an eleven-year-old will learn to keep her dad in the dark about anything having to do with boys just to avoid the hassle. Not a good scene to set for adolescence. Besides, dads who do that miss out on seeing their daughters sparkle in the light of being liked.

We're not suggesting you encourage her to bring boys home. Just honor where she is on that 1-through-17 scale on pages 140–142. A few pointers:

My dad has had to let go of me in so many ways. His love for me hasn't changed, though, and I know it never will.

Mini-Women

My dad's example will definitely have an influence on what kind of guy I choose to marry. In fact, I sometimes notice character traits in my crushes that remind me of my father. Kinda scary.

Don't intimidate every little boy who comes around. His presence
doesn't call for the third degree. He's ten.

Welcome her boy friends the same way you do her girl friends.
Don't make a big deal out of the fact that he's a boy.

Don't ask about her "boyfriend" in front of her friends.

Don't make a joke out of the whole thing, especially if she comes to
you with a problem. This is not to say you shouldn't handle it
with a sense of humor. You're toast without that. Just don't make
fun of her and minimize the importance of this in her mind.

Don't ask her why she isn't into boys, as if there's something
wrong with that.

If your daughter shows signs of being boy crazy or wants to hang
out with her big brother's friends or gets overly emotional about a
"breakup," those are definitely things you and her mom will want
to address with her—but even that can be done with kindness and
respect. We've said it before. There is always a reason for the way
a young person behaves. Something has convinced her that to feel
worthwhile, she has to work to get the attention of boys. Who knows?
Maybe that something is just a need for more from you.

We wave the biggest caution flag of all at being overprotective
when it comes to the boy scene. In this case, we mean prohibiting her
from talking to or about boys at all. As we've said before, that kind
of uber-shielding tells her you don't trust her or that she's too weak
to take care of herself even in small ways. Most of the time, when
dads go all Secret Service in this area, it's because they're afraid their
daughters will buy into the sexualized culture and start participating in it at age twelve. Yours won't if you work with her to both gain
personal strength against peer pressure and find ways to change her
world's attitudes. She's in very little danger of being taken advantage of by her eleven-year-old boy peer, so why not grab this opportunity to teach her how to be around boys and command respect,
rather than build a wall around her? Help her choose media that
portray women as equals while developing their special feminine
traits. Teach her how to manage money. Show her how to stand up
for herself without coming across as shrill. Do whatever you can to

make her strong so that she doesn't have to miss out on healthy fun with boys because you're sure something bad is going to happen to her. Your rules should be about *her* safety and well-being, not about *your* control and fear.

Show her how she should expect to be treated by a man. Actually, you do this automatically, without even realizing it. However you treat her now, that's the standard she'll go by when she begins to have relationships with guys. If you treat her like a lady, she'll want boys to do the same. If you're distant with her, only talking to her when she's done something wrong or you want her to get to some chore, she'll learn to be coy and manipulative to get the attention she wants from men. If you don't provide the best for her, she won't expect it from other guys. Says Joe Kelly, an author and blogger who is raising two tween girls on his own: "You still have the potent position of 'first man,' setting the norm of manliness for her, a norm that ultimately can be stronger than what anyone else tells her, including the hyper-sexualized message of our culture and media."[2] Domestic violence groups have even begun to use daddy-daughter dances as a preventative program, giving dads a chance to show a daughter that she deserves respect from her future boyfriends and husband. As a tween girl twirls around the floor in Dad's arms, wearing the corsage he picked out for her, she's gaining a healthy sense of how a man should cherish her.

Basically, you're the one your daughter will compare every boy to. Are you the kind of man you want your daughter to like, date, marry? You're setting the standard.

That should scare you to death, dude.

Bridging the Gap

Father, I know I'm not always the man my daughter needs for me to be as her guide to boys now and as her model for the kind of guy you want for her in her future. So please, bridge the gap between what she needs from me and what I have to give. Can't do it without you. Counting on you, Father.

Amen.

Mini-Women

My dad has always been there for me, always trying to understand. Even though sometimes he just totally doesn't get it, I always know he wants to help me. My dad loves me, and that makes up for all the mistakes he's made.

Epilogue

Being a Good Enough Dad

This was a hard book to help write. The more I thought back to Marijean's tween days, the more I thought, *I wasn't the daddy I could have been*. A lot of what I've suggested to you is based on the questions I still ask myself—

Did I spend enough time with her?
Did I answer enough of her questions?
Did I tell her often enough that she was a beautiful, gifted, unique person?
Did I show her enough that I loved her?

But I have to say that there have been standout times when I knew something I'd done was enough.

When Marijean came to me in her teens and said, "You were right, Dad. I have to be careful what kinds of situations I put myself in."
When she thanked us for teaching her social skills because she was seeing kids in her college who didn't even know how to behave in a restaurant.
When she asked us to walk her through her early divorce and blew me away with her integrity and strength under heartbreaking circumstances.
When she remarried, a good man, and said this time she wanted a marriage like her mom and I have.
When she asked me to build a crib for my soon-to-be-born grandchild.

Whenever I start beating myself up over where I fell short, I read this email my daughter sent me recently.

"You and I, we've never been so much with the touchy-feely emotional stuff," she wrote. "It's not that I don't think, or ever doubted, that you love me, and it's not that we don't tell each other that we love each other, either. There's just no spelling it out, and no cuddly, huggy-kissy stuff."

And then in true Marijean fashion, she did spell it out.

"We definitely struggled to get along at times from my childhood until I was about seventeen. But you always had an uncanny sense of what was going on with me, what I needed. You even shop for me better than Mom does."

She went on to explain why she thought we struggled "about 50 percent of the time," and her insights are right on. We did great left to our own devices, but when Mom was there, we both competed over her because she was the one who brought out the best in both of us, and we both wanted to be important. And, of course, we were so much alike—jumping right onto the "negative" emotions like anger—we were bound to bang heads. But she came to a healing realization:

"When I finally learned that emotions like anger aren't all bad, I could start to view myself and then you in a different light. And I could start to realize that you and I were never going to relate the way Mom and I relate, and that that's okay."

How, in her eyes, *did* we relate?

"When I think about you, I think about power, and action, and know-how. You're the person I want when my car breaks down, when I have to go to the ER, when our tree falls on our neighbor's house. I know you love me because I know you would protect and take care of me no matter what. If I were kidnapped, you would find me. If my leg got broken in the woods, you would splint it and carry me to civilization, even though your back is so messed up it's hard for you to get up out of chairs. I believe that men are supposed to be like you—resourceful, good in a crisis, knowledgeable about an impossible range of things, funny, ready to kill and die for me. I think I really believe you could build your own parachute and jump out of a burning high-rise building and land safely on the ground after shooting down the helicopter full of bad guys. Is it hero worship? Yeah, I guess it is. Is it realistic? Not totally, but it's not totally unfounded either. I mean, come on, you DO know how to do that stuff. Plus build houses and make fine furniture and wire electronics and fix cars and cut down trees and drive boats and tie knots and cook food and use a sewing machine and light a stage and sing and act and sneak up on people and play every sport and survive in the snow and ..."

Didn't I tell you daughters watch everything you do? And just for the record, I can't build my own parachute and land safely on the ground after shooting down a helicopter full of bad guys. But I like that she thinks I can.

She still wasn't done. (She seldom is.) "I think there were lots of times you weren't there when I was a kid," she wrote, "and I think we had a lot of needless fights and tensions. I don't really want to spend time anymore thinking about what kind of father you could have been. You did and do so much better than so many other people's dads. Despite being gone a lot, or the majority of our phone conversations consisting of 'You wanna talk to your mom?' you're not emotionally distant, and you never were. You're not Absent Dad. You're not Apathetic Dad. You're the opposite of that. You're Super-Intense Dad. You're Super-Competent Dad. That kind of comes in small doses, and now I think it's better that way. You're the dad who's there when I need you, but you raised me not to need you all the time. Mom raised me to be self-loving and self-expressive. You raised me to be self-sufficient."

There's always a slight pause there while I get a paper towel and blow my nose before I can finish reading.

"I love and respect you more than almost anyone else in the world, Dad. I feel loved by you, and that you're proud of me, and that you accept me for who I am. I fantasize about what an awesome grandfather you're going to be. I watch you and Mom getting older, and it scares me to death because it's been the three of us for a really long time, and I really don't know what I'm going to do when you're both gone. If Mom goes first and you go all weird and disappear into the Caribbean like you always say you would, I will find you. I will low-jack you. One day your Corona is going to make you really sleepy and then you're going to wake up with a microchip under your skin and a note that says, "Would it KILL you to call me?"

That part about us not being into the "touchy-feely emotional stuff." Yeah, she got that right. And yet this tribute to the flawed, short-fused father who raised her is enough to reassure me that the trying and the praying and the doing-the-best-I-could made a difference in who she is still becoming.

It's going to be the same for you. You're going to make mistakes raising your daughter. She may go through a period where she's convinced everything you did was a mistake. But if you love her and know her and accept her and teach her what wisdom you have—and do it with your own unique set of strong suits and personal challenges—you're going to have a relationship with her that is real, one that won't fade when she moves on to create her life beyond your house.

We hope this book in some way helps you to get there. If you take away nothing else from it, please carry this with you: You are the main man in your daughter's life right now, right this very minute. She needs your best. Whatever you do, make it count.

It will be enough.

Blessings,

Jim and Nancy Rue

Acknowledgments

We Didn't Do It Alone . . .

Just in case you're the kind of guy who actually reads acknowledgments, there are some people we'd like you to know about—people who believed, supported, and contributed while we were working on *What Happened to My Little Girl?*

Sandra Vander Zicht, at Zondervan, who caught our vision and made it possible.

In fact, **the whole Zondervan team—Kristi Arbogast, Robin Geelhoed, Don Gates, Bob Hudson, Jane Haradine, and Michelle Lenger**—who prove that even two people can't write a book without help (at least a *publishable* one).

Agent **Lee Hough** (no, not FBI, CIA, or NCIS—we're talking *literary* agent) who not only handled the financials and logistics but spurred us on with comments like, "Jim, you're now an author among all your other exploits. Who knew?"

The dads who shared their stories—Terry Esau, Ken Schubert, Brad Wathne, David Deal, Bruce Nuffer, and Dale McElhinney. Awesome fathers, all.

The tween girls on Nancy's blogs, **Tween You and Me** and **In Real Life**, who grounded us with the insights you'll find in "Out of the Mouths of Mini-Women." They are the true experts.

Finally, our daughter, **Marijean**, who has delighted and challenged us all her life and has made us richer, better people than we ever would have been without her. (And Brian, we know you're going to be an amazing dad to our granddaughter, the newest mini-woman.)

God's blessings on all of you.

Notes

Chapter One — Can Somebody Tell Me What's Going On?

1. David L. Siegel, Timothy J. Coffey, Gregory Livingston, *The Great Tween Buying Machine: Capturing Your Share of the Multibillion Dollar Tween Market* (Chicago: Dearborn Trade, 2004), i.

2. Maria Halkias, in reference to C&S research data in EPM Communication's Tween Spending and Influence Report, "Retailers Pinning Hopes on Edgy Tween Fashions," *Dallas Morning News*, April 10, 2010.

3. Terry Esau, in a conversation on July 7, 2008, in Orlando, Fla. Terry is the author of *Surprise Me: A 30-Day Faith Experiment* (Colorado Springs: NavPress: 2005), and, while not a parenting book, it offers a great challenge for any man.

4. Shanna Jayson, "So Cool! Tweens are emerging generation," *Today*, February 4, 2009.

5. Ibid.

6. Jason Tripp, "Keep Her Connected," December 14, 2009. *Solar Crash: http://SolarCrash.com/2009/12/keep-her-connected/.* Accessed June 18, 2010.

7. Roger Entner, "Under-aged Texting: Usage and Actual Cost," January 27, 2010. *NielsenWire: http://blog.nielsen.com/nielsenwire/online–mobile/under-aged-texting-usage-and-actual-cost/.*

8. Scott MacGregor, "Dad Power: Take a Stand!" *Daughters.com: www.Daughters.com/article/?id=82.* Accessed June 20, 2010.

9. Robert Beeson, "2010". *iShine: http://iSHinelive.com.* Accessed June 10, 2010.

10. Jayson, "So Cool!"

11. Girl Scout Research Institute, "Study Confirms: Tweens Today Are Headed in the Right Direction," "Good Intentions: The Beliefs and Values of Teens and Tweens Today." *Girl Scouts: www.girlscouts.org/research/pdf/good_intentions-full-report.pdf).* Accessed June 19, 2010.

12. Joe Kelly, "Dads Are More Than Walking Wallets." *The Dad Man: www.thedadman.com.* Accessed June 16, 2010.

13. Jeanne Elium and Don Elium, *Raising a Daughter: Parents and the Awakening of a Healthy Woman* (Berkeley, Calif.: Celestials Arts, 2003), 302.

14. Ibid., 27.

15. Paul Plant, "Fathers and Daughters," March 2010. *Today's Parent: www.todaysparent.com/teen/behaviordevelopment/article.jsp?content=20100112–135943–9556&page=.* Accessed June 16, 2010.

16. Joe Kelly, "For Dads of Tween and Teen Daughters." *The Dad Man: www.thedadman.com/dads-of-tween-and-teen-daughters.* Accessed June 16, 2010.

17. Terry Esau, conversation.

Chapter Two — What Happened to My Little Girl?

1. Inspired by Joe Kelly, *www.thedadman.com*, although we've come up with our own statements.

2. Christine Palumbo, "Good Sense Eating: Dad's influence on eating," May 24, 2010. *ChicagoParent: www.chicagoparent.com/magazines/chicago-parent/2010-june/columns/dad's-influence-on-eating.* Accessed June 16, 2010. Palumbo is referring to a 2008 study done by the *Journal for Specialists in Pediatric Nursing.*

3. Ibid.

4. Ibid.

5. Mary Jo Rapini, "Of Dads and Daughters: Fighting the Ride of Eating Disorders," June 22, 2009. *Good Therapy.org: www.GoodTherapy.org.* Accessed June 12, 2010.

6. Michael Sokolove, *Warrior Girls: Protecting Our Daughters Against the Injury Epidemic in Women's Sports* (New York: Simon & Schuster, 2008), 189.

7. National Health and Nutrition Examination Survey, 2005. *Centers for Disease Control and Prevention: www.cdc.gov/nchs/data/nhanes/survery_content_99_10.pdf.*

8. Jean Elium and Don Elium, *Raising a Daughter: Parents and the Awakening of a Healthy Woman* (Berkley Calif.: Celestial Arts, 2003), 70.

9. Hugo Schwyzer, "Boys, fathers, teasing, and disordered eating, June 6, 2008. *Hugo Schwyzer: http://HugoSchwyzer.net.* Accessed June 15, 2010.

10. Shanna Jayson, "So Cool! Tweens Are Emerging Generaton," *Today,* February 4, 2009.

Chapter Three — She'll Be Crying in a Minute

1. Jean Elium and Don Elium, *Raising a Daughter: Parents and the Awakening of a Healthy Woman* (Berkley Calif.: Celestial Arts, 2003), 19.

2. Amy Lynch with Dr. Linda Ashford, *How Can You Say That?* (Middleton, Wis.: Pleasant, 2003), 22.

3. Ibid.

4. Ibid., 20.

5. Ibid.

6. Anne Moir and David Jessel, *Brain Sex: The Real Difference between Men and Women* (New York: Delta, 1991), 2.

7. Ann Kring, "Sex Differences in Emotion: Expression, Experience, and Physiology," *Journal of Personality and Social Psychology* 74, no. 3 (March 1998): 686–703.

8. Daniel Goleman, *Emotional Intelligence: Why It Can Matter More than IQ* (New York: Bantam, 1995), 32.

9. "Tween Issue: She Wants to Shave Her Legs," January 21, 2009. *The Stir Bloggers: http://thestir.cafemom.com/search.php?keyword=She+wants+to+shave+her+legs*. Accessed June 15, 2010.

10. Elium and Elium, *Raising a Daughter*, 21.

11. Ibid.

12. Lynch with Ashford, *How Can You Say That?* 10–11.

13. Susan Brownmiller, *Femininity* (New York: Simon & Schuster, 1983), 120–21.

14. Lynch with Ashford, *How Can You Say That?* 38.

Chapter Four — We Need Another Bathroom

1. Donna Fish, "Tweens and Body Image: The Real Deal," June 1, 2009. *The Huffington Post: www.huffingtonpost.com*.

2. Jean Elium and Don Elium, *Raising a Daughter: Parents and the Awakening of a Healthy Woman* (Berkley Calif.: Celestial Arts, 2003), 327.

Chapter Five — Who Is She Today?

1. Michael Sokolove, *Warrior Girls: Protecting Our Daughters Against the Injury Epidemic in Women's Sports* (New York: Simon & Schuster, 2008), 226.

2. "Teaching Tweens Simplicity," August 12, 2008. *OnSimplicity.net*. Accessed June 24, 2010.

Chapter Six — Dealing with Girl Drama

1. Nancy Rue, *Mom's Ultimate Guide to the Tween Girl World* (Grand Rapids, Mich.: Zondervan, 2010), 217–18.

2. Mary Field Belenky, Blythe McVicker Clinchy, Nancy Rule Goldberger, and Jill Mattuck Tarule, *Women's Ways of Knowing: The Development of Self, Voice, and Mind* (New York: Harper Collins, 1996), 18.

3. Jean Elium and Don Elium, *Raising a Daughter: Parents and the Awakening of a Healthy Woman* (Berkley Calif.: Celestial Arts, 2003), 76.

4. Rosalind Wiseman, *Queen Bees and Wannabes: Helping Your Daughter Survive Cliques, Gossip, Boyfriends, and the New Realities of Girl World* (New York: Crown, 2002).

5. Rue, *Mom's Ultimate Guide*, 222.

6. Michele Borba, *Nobody Likes Me, Everybody Hates Me: The Top 25 Friendship Problems and How to Solve Them* (San Francisco: Jossey-Bass, 2005), 96.

7. Committee for Children, "Steps to Respect: Review of Research." *Committee for Children: www.cfchildren.org/media/files/str−research−foundations .pdf.* Accessed July 1, 2010.

8. *Journal of Pediatrics*, 2006.

9. Ibid.

10. Mary Dixon LeBeau, "Dealing with Mean Girls," November 9, 2009. *KABOOSE: http://parenting.kaboose.com/family-dynamics/mean-girls .html.* Accessed June 16, 2010.

Chapter Seven — I Liked It Better When Boys Had Cooties

1. Bryan Greeson, "Is Your Tween Going Out? You Better Be Joining In," April 27, 2007. *Fathers.com: www.fathers.com/content/index.php?option= com−content&task=view&id=175&Itemid=62.* Accessed June 15, 2010.

2. Joe Kelly, "For Dads of Tween and Teen Daughters." *The Dad Man: www. thedadman.com\dads−of−tween−and−teen−daughters.* Accessed June 16, 2010.